Desktop Publishing
in the University

Desktop Publishing in the University

edited by

Joan N. Burstyn

The 5/91
Boston
Computer
Society

One Center Plaza

Boston,

Massachusetts

02108

school of education
SYRACUSE UNIVERSITY

Distributed by Syracuse University Press

First Edition 1991

91 92 93 94 95 96 97 98 99   6 5 4 3 2 1

Library of Congress Cataloging-in-Publication Data

Desktop publishing in the university / edited by Joan N. Burstyn

p. cm.
Includes index.
ISBN 0-8156-8116-X $\mathcal{I}$, $\mathcal{B}$
1. Scholarly publishing—Data processing.
2. Universities and colleges—Communications systems.
3. College publications—Data processing.
4. University presses—Automation.
5. Desktop publishing.
I. Burstyn, Joan N.
II. Syracuse University. School of Education.
Z286.S37D47   1991   91-8759
686.2' 2544'0285—dc20

Manufactured in the United States of America

CONTENTS

One Center Plaza

Boston,

Massachusetts

02108

ACKNOWLEDGMENTS

I wish to thank colleagues from across the country, particularly those who attended the March 1989 conference on "The Impact of Desktop Publishing on University Life" sponsored by Syracuse University and the Association of American University Presses, for encouraging me to edit this book. The conference provided a springboard for discussion where Robert M. Hayes, Robert L. Oakman, David May, Robert J. Silverman, Deborah G. Johnson, and Czeslaw Jan Grycz presented earlier versions of their chapters. In the book, other contributors write on issues not raised at the conference, including some that have surfaced only within the last two years. I prepared the manuscript while on a semester's leave provided by Syracuse University.

I wish also to thank many people at Syracuse University: especially Dean Steven T. Bossert, for enabling the book to be published by the School of Education; David May and his staff in Publications, Printing, and Graphic Services: Margaret McComb, George Lowery, and Christopher O. Purcell, for producing and designing the book on desktop publishing equipment; and Charles Backus and the staff of Syracuse University Press, for its promotion and distribution.

Joan N. Burstyn
Syracuse University
January 1991

"Desktop Publishing: Its Impact on the Academic Community" is reprinted by permission of University of Toronto Press from *Scholarly Publishing* (October 1989), pp. 57-63.

Desktop Publishing
in the University

Introduction: The Promise of Desktop Publishing

By Joan N. Burstyn

This book provides scholars and administrators at universities and colleges with information for intelligent decision-making on the impact of desktop publishing. Designed as an investigation of the new technology's implications, not as a how-to book, its purpose is to engage readers in discussion about the ethical, economic, and structural implications of desktop publishing for higher education.

In 1985, when one of the first books on the technology was published, the term desktop publishing described the whole spectrum of electronic publishing. Manufacturers then began to segment their marketing. They reserved the term desktop publishing for the process leading to hard copy text produced from computer, printer, and software for graphics, text, and page layout. They ignored other forms of desktop publishing because, at that time, they did not have any hot products to exploit. To provide readers with a broad perspective of the new technology's potential, in this book we reaffirm the inclusive meaning of desktop publishing, referring at times to the whole range of electronic publishing and its influence on scholarly communication. Rather than discussing only the production of hard copy from computerized text, we include nonprint products and the potential for developing fluid texts transmitted, added to, and amended electronically without a final printed product.

The marketing areas of desktop publishing that took off in 1985 affected the design of ephemeral advertising materials, such as brochures, catalogs, magazines, and posters, and the design of materials for educational courses, seminars, and workshops. Scholarly research benefited from some of these products, but manufacturers at first paid little attention to developing software especially for scholars.

Market segmentation has now made desktop publishing a well-defined subset of electronic publishing. Since

*Joan N.
Burstyn*

its largest impact is in marketing and advertising, manufacturers of desktop publishing equipment are well-placed to further the marketing and advertising of their own products. However, the intricate link between desktop publishing and marketing and advertising may be disadvantageous to developing the more revolutionary potential of electronic publishing, those other forms whose end product is not a book, a brochure, or a poster.

Electronic media lend themselves to innovative products. Indeed, business and industry already use these innovations for maintenance of inventory, financial transactions, transportation of goods, and monitoring of manufacturing processes. In the last decade, such innovations revolutionized much of business and industry. Desktop publishing in its broadest sense is part of that revolution, a mechanism for transmitting information to new audiences through new media. The rules that govern discourse for those media have yet to be decided. By examining the potential of desktop publishing to revolutionize aspects of the work of universities and colleges, the authors of this book hope to further the discussion in higher education on the rules that we want to govern our discourse about electronic media.

Marketing and Distributing Desktop Publications

Several writers below define what desktop publishing is. One, limiting himself to the narrow version of the term, calls it an oxymoron—"a seeming self-contradiction"—because it refers to desktop *printing* and not to *publishing*, which includes the marketing and distribution of what has been printed. Though this argument has been made before, nothing has stopped the application of the term *publishing* to the process of desktop printing. We may shudder at its inappropriateness, but we cannot stop its adoption as a common term.

However, the distinction is a crucial one. The task of finding a market for one's work, and then providing that market with goods in a timely manner, is important. Publishers have traditionally done far more than merely design and print books. Their continued livelihood depends on sales; therefore, a large portion of their budget and their energy is devoted to advertising, marketing, and distribution. Any technology that offers authors both alternatives to printing through a conventional press and, at the same time, marketing and distribution potential, appears particularly threatening to publishers. What remains to be seen is whether authors will be willing to invest the effort needed to publish themselves effectively using the new technology.

It was the advent of the copy machine, however, not desktop publishing, that first threatened the markets of both commercial and university presses. Copy machines threatened them in two ways. The first made it possible for people interested in some but not all of a book to reproduce that part from a library copy and thereby avoid purchasing the book. The second made it possible for people or organizations to reproduce typewritten or even printed material themselves at an affordable price for private distribution. As Robert Hayes points out elsewhere in this book, ephemeral reports, surveys, essays, and other literature have mushroomed in the last three decades.

Desktop publishing produced a new subset of ephemeral materials. The sheer volume of desktop publishing exacerbates problems that already exist for all ephemeral printed materials: How can all these materials be catalogued, indexed, and classified? That issue is discussed below. And how can material produced on the desktop be marketed and distributed effectively? Developing new ways to market and distribute materials produced on the desktop is an urgent task if desktop publishing is to flourish in academia.

The marketing and distribution of electronic materials call for innovative structures, not the adaptation of old ones. In the narrow sense of desktop publishing, innovators might develop businesses to be clearing houses for the printed materials created by individual authors through desktop publishing. Such businesses could be an extension of existing cooperative distribution services among university presses, for instance. However, in the broader sense of desktop publishing, marketing and distribution fall under electronic bulletin boards, E-mail, and electronic shopping. The conventional notions of distributing

*Joan N.
Burstyn*

and marketing books and journals become moot when I, at my desktop, can send my product wherever I wish electronically.

One writer suggests that we must include, as desktop publishing, not only printed material but also material that is circulated by E-mail and by magnetic disk, including CD-ROM (Compact Disk—Read Only Memory) and WORM (Write Once, Read Many), because they are produced on the desktop and have the potential of being widely distributed. These issues are addressed again in a chapter on scholarly communication, where we explore the development of electronic journals and the problems associated with their marketing and distribution. If academic freedom and access to the scholarly record for all who wish it are to be maintained, new ways for marketing and distributing the results for electronically produced scholarship must be developed.

Archiving Desktop Publications

Desktop publishing has already caused an explosion of new publications. Many are not archived and therefore cannot be retrieved by scholars for future reference. Material printed only when individuals download it from bulletin boards or E-mail is difficult to archive and verify. New questions arise: What should be archived? If authors send an electronic text by E-mail to a group of colleagues or place it on an electronic bulletin board, have they published it? What does peer review mean for electronic texts? If a text changes as individuals comment on it or add their own thoughts to it, who is the author? In an electronic environment, how does one know when a text becomes final? Who pays for cataloging the new ephemeral literature? What organizations do the work? Until we find answers to these questions, scholars will hesitate to use electronic media for fear of bypassing the controls they have devised for measuring the quality of each other's work.

In his recent book, *The Librarian, the Scholar, and the Future of the Research Library*, Eldred Smith suggests that computers provide libraries with an unprecedented opportunity to preserve the whole of the scholarly record, rather than merely part of it. He claims that preservation is crucial to the integrity of scholarship, and that the mechanisms devised over several centuries to maintain and preserve the quality of scholarly research have to be adapted to an electronic environment.[1] However, his vision of a permanent, storable scholarly record may become outdated as the use of electronic communication spreads.

Technology and Change

We may be tempted to believe that technologies in themselves cause change. But, as Deborah Johnson points out in her book *Computer Ethics*, that is a simplistic analysis.[2] Technologies are always introduced into some existing environment that may be receptive or antagonistic to them. Some institutions in an environment favor their use; others do not. The power of any technology will then be constrained or expanded according to the power of the welcoming institutions. Change is brought about by the subtle interaction of technology, institutions, and individuals who wish to see changes in their environment.

Each party to the changes—the people, the technology, and the environment—places its own limitations on them. In the use of a new technology, people are limited by their own imaginations as well as by the constraints of the machinery with which they interact. Since new images and metaphors take time to evolve, we can say with confidence that any impact desktop publishing has now is dwarfed by its potential impact in the future.

Many people, for instance, use the computer as they did a typewriter, only superficially exploring the power of the machine for innovative tasks. That's because people require time to develop innovative applications of new technologies. When they do develop such applications, they find that some technologies influence society more profoundly than others. The technology of the wheel, for instance, had a profound influence on cultures, affecting even the concept of personal property. By making it easier for humans to transfer belongings from one place to another, the wheel encouraged people to acquire new kinds and amounts of personal property.[3]

Joan N.
Burstyn

The environment always shapes the ways one uses a technology, determining who will have control of a technology and who will have access to it. Copy machines, for instance, may liberate individuals in a society that encourages their personal use. But they do not liberate individuals in a society where access to them is tightly controlled, and where official note is taken of each item copied.

However, over time a technology such as the copy machine will interact with any environment to change it in subtle ways. These changes may well involve structural changes as well as changes in interpersonal dynamics, as Shoshana Zuboff demonstrated effectively in her study of the effect of introducing computers into several industries.[4] Once installed, with all the trappings of bureaucracy carefully delineated so as to prevent radical change, new technologies can still transform a system.

The question arises, who is to control such transformation? Can we choose between alternative futures? Can we plan the changes we would like to occur? Can we prevent those changes we feel would be detrimental to the working environment of the university, for instance?

Those were the questions we asked in 1987 as we began to plan for a conference on "The Impact of Desktop Publishing on University Life."[5] Two years later, when the conference took place, we faced another question: Who are *we*? At the conference we fell into two groups: those who liked the ways scholarly communication was traditionally conducted and those who wanted to see the old ways changed. These two groups reflect the institutional responses to new technologies referred to above. This book, therefore, includes ideas from both groups of people as they contemplate the changes wrought by desktop publishing. Some of the book's authors attended the conference, others did not. The chapters have been selected to express a variety of views of the impact of desktop publishing on universities.

Two Perspectives on Desktop Publishing and Universities

There are two perspectives provided by the people at the Syracuse conference and other scholars. Those who like the way scholarly communication has traditionally been conducted find in the new technology an extension of the old. Computers running page-layout software assist with tasks that have always been tedious and time consuming. Cost savings will result. There is no need, however, to subvert a whole structure to obtain them. The task of university press personnel, for instance, is to tell authors to hold their horses rather than to allow them free rein with the new technology on their desktops. Scholars will have to adapt existing mechanisms to monitor the quality of scholarly research, just as librarians will have to adapt new ways to preserve the scholarly record and make it available to scholars.

Those who want the old ways changed see universities on the cusp of a new world. They speak not only about new ways to organize known tasks, but of new kinds of human interactions and new ways to construct knowledge. They are less concerned than the other group about maintaining established controls, since such controls have often maintained the status quo rather than furthered scholarship.

New Ways to Construct Knowledge

Digital fusion, which stores text and graphics together, forces one to think pictorially; it uses new metaphors that we, with our orientation to print, are not used to. We have not yet evolved the vocabulary with which to describe the work we have to do. The very words with which we think about the issue are inappropriate. The word vocabulary, for instance, refers to the spoken and written *word*—we do not have a way to express the combined word-image that we need to construct new metaphors.

When the image and the word can be created, stored, and retrieved simultaneously, we have revolutionized the tools that human beings have to understand the world. Marshall McLuhan provided a way to describe the scope of such changes when he wrote: "The 'message' of any medium or technology is the change of scale or pace or pattern that it introduces into human affairs."[6] To fully understand the message of desktop publishing, we must consider it as part of the change of scale, pace, and pattern in human affairs brought about by the computer.

Joan N.
Burstyn

New Job Descriptions and New Curricula

What changes can we envision within the university? The first areas influenced by the new technology have been public relations and printing services, and university presses. We include here chapters by people from both areas. They describe two interlinking changes: in authority structures and in job descriptions. Both these changes may be threatening to some people. Susan Gubernat, editor-in-chief of the magazine *Publish!*, suggested that most people threatened by desktop publishing belong to a craft that depends upon years of acquired expertise. According to Gubernat, the new collaboration desktop publishing demands from designers and editors can be exhilarating for both. However, employers have to spend money to assist their employees as they adapt to change. Because learning curves are steep, it is profitable financially and also desirable for the well-being of the employees for them to receive training in their new tasks.[7]

The curricula of university programs in journalism and graphic design are also changing as a result of the changes in authority structures and in job descriptions for editors and designers. According to Judith Burton, change in journalism has been slow, in part because developing courses in desktop publishing depends upon faculty members who have a personal interest in the field. Few universities provide programs, or released time, for faculty members to train in the advanced use of the new technology. At the same time, departments find it difficult to keep abreast of newly marketed hardware and software.[8]

Nevertheless, while some university departments have been slow to respond to the demand from business for employees with desktop publishing experience, others have responded with alacrity. The journalism department at California State University at Northridge, for instance, created a desktop computer lab with money allocated from the state lottery. In 1987 it began a practicum in desktop publishing, using campus units as the clients. The results benefited students and clients alike.[9]

In this book, we do not include any study of the changes taking place in the nature of the work done by book designers. Such a study, similar to the one undertaken for several other occupations by Shoshana Zuboff in her book *In the Age of the Smart Machine*, would be timely indeed. Are book designers experiencing a similar loss of physical contact, of hands-on control, as skilled workers in pulp factories, for instance? Or has their work always been sufficiently "intellective"[10] that the switch from manual layout to computer design has not disrupted their cognitive operations?

Instead, we report some broad changes taking place, the rationale for them, and some observations on the impact of those changes on university operations.

None of the changes in jobs or curricula described above has effected a change in the product—be it a brochure, poster, catalog, or annual report. Only the process of production has changed. Desktop publishing in its original sense included all of electronic publishing, however. It seems likely that while traditional products will persist, they may become obsolete as writers, editors, and designers turn their attention to fluid on-screen creations more like videos and TV commercials.

New Approaches to Faculty Publications

The changes we already see are merely the tip of an iceberg. Below the surface is the potential of electronic communication to tear apart dichotomies that have governed academic life for decades: teaching and research, text and commentary, and the published and the unpublished word. Whether these dichotomies are torn apart, or whether they remain despite the new technologies, will depend upon decisions that university faculties make in the next few years.

Some scholars feel that the dichotomy in universities between teaching and research has become a destructive force. Undergraduates complain that faculty members care only about their research and not about their teaching. Excellent researchers have sometimes been retained and even promoted whatever their record of teaching, while excellent teachers have sometimes not been promoted and been dismissed when they failed to meet the research criteria for tenure.[11] Faculty members themselves feel torn between the conflicting demands of teaching and re-

Joan N.
Burstyn

search. The tension is particularly strong for those faculty members who believe teaching to be an important task for a professor.[12]

By enabling faculty members to engage in teaching and research at the same time, electronic communication could abolish this dichotomy. And it could bring a new democracy between the faculty and students through a mutual experience of commenting on one another's research and writing. For a long while, scientists have included graduate students on research projects, who comment on drafts of reports and articles, and sometimes even draft major sections. In the social sciences such an inclusionary policy has been less extensive, but nevertheless it exists. And, as in the sciences, the unit of research reported in a scholarly paper in the social sciences has become smaller and smaller, enabling those involved with a particular project to obtain as many publications from it as possible.[13] With the advent of electronic publishing, even larger numbers of people can comment on and add to scholarly papers. Therefore more students will be taught the skills of commenting on and editing the written word. Faculty members will have to provide students with more guidance in commenting and editing than they do now to ensure that academic standards may be maintained and even improved.

In some disciplines, such as literature and philosophy, electronic communication may break down the dichotomy between text and commentary as well. In an activity called *Philo's Workshop*, philosopher Thomas F. Green engages his students and colleagues in an electronic conversation around specific texts. The purpose of the workshop is for participants to engage in language concept analysis. They comment on texts selected by Philo (one of two aliases used by Green in the workshop) and elaborate on each other's comments about them.

> Although the text for the class is available on the computer, the text is ever-changing, unlike a textbook. As students, we have a say in determining what issues to discuss and from which angle. We in essence "control" our own educational process....The computer also gives us control

over time. Philo allows conversation to continue past the scheduled class time of Tuesdays, 4:00–7:00 p.m. Individual classes essentially gather whenever we can fit the time in our schedules (even at 1 a.m. on a Saturday morning!).[14]

The conversation may be ongoing, without end. And thus the commentary on a particular text and on the comments about the commentary itself may be forever changing.

By commenting on each other's texts, we create an evolving class text. Together we grope towards understanding, towards entering the formal mode of discourse. Each of us provides a hand to guide the other. The texts are alive in us, and shaped and molded by us.[15]

At what point, then, does a new commentary become final? Only, one might suggest, when some arbitrary time limit is imposed upon the discussion. Only when some external demand for assessment of progress is placed upon the participants.

Not every electronic discussion is as structured as *Philo's Workshop*, nor does it produce good writing. Material on electronic bulletin boards often contains chit-chat, more akin to conversation over coffee than to discussion at professional meetings. From the descriptions of students in *Philo's Workshop*, it is clear that a skillful facilitator can design rules for electronic discussion that significantly enhance students' processes of thinking. Similarly, some teleconferences establish rules that enhance the learning of those who participate; others allow the discussions to wander fruitlessly.

Advantages and Drawbacks to Electronic Communication

In one chapter, Robin Peek and I discuss the potential of desktop publishing (in its inclusive sense) to enhance scholarly communication. Here I examine in more detail some advantages and drawbacks to it that exist today.

In Fall 1987, Syracuse University's Kellogg Project be-

Joan N.
Burstyn

gan an electronic journal, *New Horizons in Adult Education.* After two years, the editors decided to send an electronic questionnaire to the journal's readers to assess its impact and acceptance. The results were analyzed by one of the editors, Michael Erskine Ehringhaus, in a paper, "The Electronic Journal: Promises and Predicaments." Ehringhaus reported the various opinions held by scholars about electronic journals. He cited Robert J. Silverman and K.C. Green, who believe that getting professional societies, editors, and promotion and tenure committees to accept electronic journals will be difficult. He also cited those, including myself, who believe that the new technology will "have a democratizing effect, permitting scholars at smaller institutions and those with ideas outside the mainstream of a given discipline to participate more in scholarly discourse."[16]

In discussing the benefits of electronic publication, Ehringhaus calls attention to the potential of electronic networks for increasing community involvement in the creation of knowledge. Green notes that many scholars use networks to circulate drafts of articles for review and comment. As a result, peer review is transformed from a static to a dynamic process "with more opportunity and some risk for those engaging in it, and with a better outcome."[17] Silverman expands this idea in a later chapter of this book.

Another potential benefit of electronic journals is that they are not constrained by the cost of printing, and therefore they accept longer articles than print journals. However, a new constraint affects electronic journals that may turn out to be more stringent than the cost of printing: the strain most people find reading from a computer screen. Kerr, Lambert, and Robertson seem to suggest that brevity may be more appropriate for electronic media than expansiveness. However, as Ehringhaus notes:

> If screen readability is a defining aspect of an electronic journal, then it, too, becomes a defining aspect of the journal's content and substance; limiting an article in length to a certain number of screens might have an impact on how authors are able to address a particular subject. A lengthy electronic journal, while not tak-

ing advantage of the medium in terms of on-screen readability, could very well be taking advantage of the technology in other ways: broadening the avenues of dialogue and dissemination of knowledge.[18]

New Horizons in Adult Education, a refereed journal run by an international editorial board of graduate students in Adult Education (following the model of the *Harvard Educational Review*), has a small readership—it is distributed, free of charge, on BITNET through the Adult Education Network (AEDNET). At the time of the study in Spring 1989, AEDNET had 155 subscribers. Although small, the readership is international, and includes professors, students, and practitioners of adult education. Those submitting articles in the journal's first two years came from Canada, Madagascar, New Zealand, Nicaragua, Nigeria, Sweden, Syria, and Tanzania, as well as the United States.

The results of the editors' survey are merely suggestive since only 27 people, seventeen percent of the readership, responded to the electronic questionnaire. Nevertheless, the questions asked and the responses received suggest that further surveys of this kind should be made.

One set of responses dealt with "a) how knowledge moves within the field, b) the field's acceptance of a journal distributed in an alternative manner, and c) how the technical aspects of delivery may or may not affect readers' views and use of an electronic journal."[19] Of the small number of potential readers who responded, 29 percent said they scrolled through the journal on the screen, 85 percent made a paper copy of it, 29 percent passed electronic copies of the journal to others, and 54 percent passed paper copies to others. Thus the journal is reaching a wider audience than those who receive it initially. Ehringhaus did not discuss what the implications might be of copying and passing on to others a *subscription* journal. Nor did he discuss the copyright implications of making copies to pass on to others. The most perturbing response was that 36 percent of the respondents reported experiencing technical problems in receiving the journal. According to Ehringhaus:

*Joan N.
Burstyn*

The process of receiving, managing, storing, reading, manipulating, and printing lengthy electronic files requires detailed knowledge of one's particular mainframe system. Without that knowledge, reading an electronic journal can be problematic. In order to assess incidental learning, respondents were asked whether or not they had, in fact, learned more about the use of computers as the result of receiving and reading *New Horizons.*Of those who responded to the question (70 percent), 53 percent stated that they had learned something.[20]

As Ehringhaus points out later, the variety of steps each individual has to take depends on his or her particular computer system. It is, therefore, difficult for editors of an electronic journal distributed via a network such as BIT-NET to provide readers with simple instructions for accessing it. Yet Ehringhaus, as an educator of adults, thinks this is an important task. "The prospect of disseminating a journal that not only publishes the knowledge of a field but, at the same time, has a built-in structure for encouraging and facilitating technological learning is an intriguing one and could be explored in the future development of the electronic journal."[21] Since the study was conducted, bulletin boards based on micro- and minicomputers rather than mainframes, with access available through PCs rather than dumb terminals, have become more common. They now offer alternative delivery methods for electronic journals.

Not all electronic journals are included in on-line bibliographic services. A drawback discussed by readers of *New Horizons*, as well as by some authors in this book, is the lack of access through usual bibliographic channels. Readers suggested that *New Horizons* should be catalogued in ERIC. This issue is important because of the costs of cataloguing and abstracting. Only a journal that is catalogued can ensure its authors that their work will be retrievable, and therefore cited, by other scholars in the future.

Desktop Publishing and Faculty Promotion and Tenure

How will desktop publishing, in its broadest sense, affect promotion and tenure at universities and colleges? In Fall 1988, David Crismond reported that academics were divided in their answers to this question. Some felt that desktop publishing could only help faculty members add to their publications; others, while not disagreeing, felt that the value of their work would be challenged if it had not passed through the traditional channels of peer review.[22] The comments all assumed that publications were crucial for a faculty member's promotion and tenure. Now, however, there is a growing tendency for ideas to be developed and shared on bulletin boards, and through private electronic networks. Does this mean that the dichotomy between the published and unpublished word will disappear? If so, how will the productivity of faculty members be evaluated in the future? Will entry to particular networks be controlled so that one's status may be assessed by the networks to which one has access?

Will faculty become obsessed by publishing hardcopy from their desktop, so that they spend more time on the medium of delivery than they did in the past? If so, will they have less time to spend on conceptualizing new research projects? Will their productivity fall as a result? And will faculty wish to be assessed on a book's design as well as its content? "If so promotion and tenure committees may have to revise their expectations and develop new criteria by which to judge the influence of manuscript design."[23]

One could argue just as well that faculty productivity will increase, because authors will deliver manuscripts to publishers in camera-ready form, thus reducing the production time for books. If that is the case, will desktop publishing merely "up the ante," so that more, not fewer, publications will be expected of faculty members? How will faculty members deal with the explosion of new information that more printed material will generate?

From the earlier discussion of *Philo's Workshop* we can see that even more radical changes may be in store. How will promotion and tenure committees respond to the merging of research and teaching? How will they treat the

*Joan N.
Burstyn*

possibility that final products in the form of printed articles no longer exist? Or that a faculty member may hand
in hardcopy of several versions of one "article," each one
dated and acknowledging additional ideas from other
scholars?

How faculty members deal with these issues once they
become members of promotion and tenure committees
will affect how readily electronic communication is adopted by the academic community. These questions will
surely force scholars to consider why their predecessors in-
stituted specific quality controls on scholarship in the first
place, whether each such control now serves a useful purpose, and if not, whether a new type of control is needed
to replace it.

Democratization of Disciplines

Desktop publishing may affect some disciplines more
than others. University presses now use desktop publishing to produce small runs of esoteric books, where
before such runs were uneconomical. "Thus, disciplines
or topics with small audiences may now blossom in ways
unknown before. Similarly, there may be a flowering of literary genres not cultivated by previous technologies."[24]
The effect of catering to new audiences is that students
may be attracted to areas that they previously eschewed
because scholars in them had few outlets for publishing.
We recognize that it is easier to get published in some areas than others, but few academics admit that technical
and economic criteria determine which areas flourish and
which languish.

Once scholars in esoteric areas find an audience for their
work, they will be more likely to publish and thus to receive
promotion and tenure from their peers. With more students,
they will demand more resources from the university. Desktop publishing, then, has the potential to reshape the hierarchy of power among disciplines within the university.

Who Bears the Cost of Desktop Publishing?

In a later chapter, Charles Creesy of Princeton University Press writes about the cost saving of desktop publishing to university presses. There are indeed savings,

once the initial capital outlay for equipment has been made. Some savings come from a reduction of personnel needed to complete a book. On the other hand, some savings to university presses come from passing the cost back to the author. Similarly, some costs for publicity are passed back from public relations departments to academic departments. This reshuffling of outlay has important ramifications for university finance:

> As faculty members become aware of the technology's potential, more and more pressure is being placed on departments to purchase equipment to make desktop publications available—not only for faculty papers but for departmental newsletters, course materials, and even student-initiated productions. Capital costs are likely to pale into insignificance as the cost of supplies increases by leaps and bounds with increased usage. Like a labrador puppy, the technology's appetite is infinite.[25]

Conclusion

This book engages in discussion at the springtime of a new technology. The questions asked here may be the first shoots of a giant bean stalk. Who can tell whether electronic publishing will prove as revolutionary as the printing press? And who can tell whether it will take us centuries to understand its impact, as it has taken us five centuries to understand the impact of Gutenberg's invention? Desktop publishing, in its narrow sense, may be a way station to a greater revolution, in which we read only from a screen, never from a printed page.

We may be passing from the age of individually written works into an age of collaborative creation. In that case, the criteria we use to measure scholarly worth and by which we encourage scholars to seek individual immortality are as antiquated as the Model T is among automobiles.

The Promise of Desktop Publishing

*Joan N.
Burstyn*

NOTES

1. See Eldred Smith, *The Librarian, the Scholar, and the Future of the Research Library* (New York: Greenwood Press, 1990), especially chapters 3 and 5.

2. See Deborah G. Johnson, *Computer Ethics* (Englewood Cliffs, NJ: Prentice-Hall, Inc., 1985), chapter 5: "Computers and Power."

3. For an expansion of these ideas see Marshall McLuhan, *Understanding Media: The Extensions of Man* (New York: McGraw Hill Book Company, 1966. Original copyright 1964), pp. 93-94, and chapter 19.

4. See Shoshana Zuboff, *In the Age of the Smart Machine* (New York: Basic Books, 1988).

5. Sponsored by Syracuse University and the Association of American University Presses, an international conference titled "The Impact of Desktop Publishing on University Life" took place in Syracuse, March 13-14, 1989.

   The conference was reported in Thomas J. DeLoughry, "Scholarly Journals in Electronic Form Seen as Means to Speed Pace of Publication and Promote Dialogue," *Chronicle of Higher Education* (March 22, 1989): A11,& A16. A distillation of ideas from the conference by Jane M. Hugo titled "Electronic Publishing Puts Byte Into Academic Publishing," was published in the electronic journal *New Horizons in Adult Education* 4, no. 9/90 (Spring/Summer 1990): pp. 23-26.

6. McLuhan, *Understanding Media* (1966), p.24.

7. From Susan Gubernat, "Editing and Quality Control," remarks presented at the Conference on "The Impact of Desktop Publishing on University Life," Syracuse University, March 13, 1989.

8. See Judith Burton, "Desktop Publishing: Applications in the Classroom," in *Computer-Assisted Writing Instruction in Journalism and Professional Education*, Frederick Williams with the assistance of Gale F. Wiley, Al Hester, Judith Burton, and Jack Nolan (New York: Praeger, 1989), pp. 59-74.

9. See Maureen Shubow Rubin, "Communications: Desktop Publishing Comes to the Classroom," *Academic Computing*

(February 1988): 26-28 & 51-53.

10. Zuboff describes this new concept as follows: "As information technology restructures the work situation, it abstracts thought from action.... The thinking ... is of a different quality from the thinking that attended the display of action-centered skills. It combines abstraction, explicit inference, and procedural reasoning. Taken together, these elements make possible a new set of competencies that I call intellective skills." (*In the Age of the Smart Machine*, pp. 75-76.)

11. These issues have been taken up nationally by a recently formed student organization, Undergraduates for a Better Education. For a discussion of the tensions faculty members encounter between teaching and research see Ernest L. Boyer, *College: The Undergraduate Experience in America* (New York: Harper and Row, Publishers, 1987), chapter 8, "Faculty: Mentors and Scholars."

12. For a further discussion of this issue see, Joan N. Burstyn "The Challenge to Education from New Technology," in *Preparation for Life? The Paradox of Education in the Late Twentieth Century*, Joan N. Burstyn, ed. (London: Falmer Press, 1986), pp. 184-86.

13. See William J. Broad, "The Publishing Game: Getting More for Less," *Science* 211 (1981): 1137. On the need for scientists to establish priority of discovery, see Derek J. De Solla Price, *Little Science, Big Science* (New York: Columbia University Press, 1963),pp. 69-70. For a later discussion of this and other relevant issues, see Deana L. Astle, "The Scholarly Journal: Whence or Wither," *Journal of Academic Librarianship* 15, no. 3 (July 1989): 152.

14. Quotation from an unpublished paper, "Philo's Workshop: An Interactive Electronic Text": part 3, "The Computer as Enabler." Obtainable from T.F. Green @ SUVM.

15. Ibid., part 7, "The Seduction."

16. Joan N. Burstyn, as cited by DeLoughry, "Scholarly Journals in Electronic Form," *Chronicle of Higher Education* (March 22, 1989): A11.

17. K.C. Green, as quoted in DeLoughry, "Scholarly Journals in Electronic Form," *Chronicle of Higher Education* (March 22,

1989): A11.

18. See Michael Erskine Ehringhaus, "The Electronic Journal: Promises and Predicaments," Syracuse University Kellogg Project Occasional Paper, 1989: 5. Ehringhaus cites J. Kerr, M. Lambert, and D. Robertson, "Electronic Networking in the Post-Secondary Community: NETNORTH/BITNET," *Online Journal of Distance Education* (Fall, 1988).

19. Ehringhaus, "The Electronic Journal:" 13.

20. Ibid.: 17.

21. Ibid.: 20.

22. See David Crismond, "Desktop Publish or Perish: Administration and Faculty Are Bringing Desktop Publishing Into the University," *Publish!* (October 1988), p. 52. The article (pp. 52-57) surveys the uses of desktop publishing in higher education at that time.

23. Joan N. Burstyn, "Desktop Publishing Will Affect University Life," *Syracuse Record* 19, no. 24 (March 6, 1989): 6.

24. *Ibid.*

25. *Ibid.*

Who Should Be in Control?

By Robert M. Hayes

The Perspective of a Faculty Member

Trying to control a faculty is like trying to herd cats: all effort is counterproductive. To draw on an historic phrase, my attitude is "Let a hundred flowers bloom!"

As a faculty member, my opinion is that there should be no controls on the use of desktop publishing. The faculty member's tasks are to generate knowledge and to communicate it as widely as possible. Desktop publishing provides me, as a faculty member, with a powerful tool to meet those imperatives. To place controls on it would be to interfere with my responsibilities and even my career.

I bring to that view some specific experience. Some years ago, in two successive years, I was responsible for two conferences. The proceedings of each were, from a publishing standpoint, identical. They had the same format, the same kinds of tables and graphics, the same number of pages. For each of them, there was a complete and edited manuscript of the text of papers presented; in fact, the text served as the basis for material provided to the participants of each conference.

For the first conference, I negotiated with a commercial publisher, at the urging of a professional colleague who was editor of the series in which the volume indeed subsequently appeared. The manuscript went through the usual process of review by the publisher, both internal and external. It was accepted for publication, with some enthusiasm in fact, and so proceeded through the publication process—copy editing, typesetting, galley proof, page proof, indexing—to final publication. It took three years, from completion of the conference to final publication! Now, that was exceptionally long in my experience, but still it is not unusual for as much as two years to be required.

For the second conference, I decided to use desktop publishing. The book was available for distribution with-

*Robert M.
Hayes*

in six months! And the publication quality, including format, font, and binding was at least the equivalent of the commercially produced volume for the first conference. Furthermore, the entire production process was completely under my control so that format, the handling of tables and graphics, and the form of the index could be determined by my needs.

The implications are obvious: faster turn-around, better responsiveness, more direct control—they all add up to more effective communication of the results as I wanted them. It is no wonder that desktop publishing should be an overwhelming success, as far as the faculty member is concerned.

The Perspective of an Administrator

I have also been an academic administrator, however, for nearly thirty years; as a result, I bring the perspective of one who manages resources. Desktop publishing is by no means a trivial task. With due respect to the beauty of the Macintosh interface, it is labor intensive at every stage of the process, from data entry to formatting and design, to editing and preparing for production, to actual final publication. It is consuming of faculty members' time—as long as they find it sufficiently stimulating intellectually; but it is even more consuming of support staff and resources.

As a dean, I become concerned when faculty spend their time in nonsubstantive pursuits, and desktop publishing certainly raises that concern. I am concerned when support staff must spend their time in such activities, with reduced effectiveness in support of teaching and research. I become concerned when computing equipment becomes committed to activities not directly supportive of instruction and research.

However, during my tenure as dean I have placed no controls upon faculty use of the facilities of the school for any purposes, including desktop publishing. There has been no reason to do so, since the facilities available within the school and through general campus resources for instruction and research have been sufficient to support the demands of every kind.

Viewing these issues in the context of an entire university campus, however, I see that the problems may become monumental. Again, the implications are obvious: how do we control the use of time and resources so as to be most effective?

The Problem of Definition

All of that, indeed, is simply introductory to my real concerns, and I must now turn to some problems in definition. What is encompassed by the term desktop publishing as a process of printing? What is encompassed by the term desktop publishing as a process of publication? What is encompassed by the term control?

The Publishing Aspect of Control

I believe that desktop publishing is an oxymoron—a self-contradictory term. For many years I was affiliated with John Wiley & Sons—as editor of the Information Sciences Series and as a principal in a subsidiary engaged in publishing as part of the Wiley organization. For even more years I was an associate editor of the *Journal of the Association for Computing Machinery* (*J-ACM*). From those experiences, as well as from more general interest in publishing, I have immense respect for the importance of the publisher. Let me here briefly review the several roles the publisher plays.

First, is identifying and encouraging potential authors. In a sense, this is the most important role since it creates opportunities that might not otherwise exist. Surprisingly, even from the academic world, where publication is the life blood, there are difficulties in encouraging people to publish. Wiley, as a commercial publisher focusing on scientific, technical, and professional books and journals, depends greatly upon academic authors, but finds it difficult to identify people capable of writing good books and journal articles. Even for professional and scholarly journals, such as *J-ACM*, the number of authors and suitable articles is far less than is needed. This task of the publisher and of the editor to encourage people to publish is important and difficult; it involves constant discussion with potential authors, encouragement to them, and assistance in bringing manuscripts to a publishable state.

Robert M.
Hayes

This brings me to the second role of the publisher, quality control. That arises in the identification of authors, of course, but it also arises in creating publishable works of suitable quality. Manuscripts of books and even of scholarly articles all too often are poor in their organization, their writing, and even their substantive content. The publisher's editors bring such poor manuscripts to a quality that justifies publishing. The processes of internal and external review, copy editing, and preparation for publication all serve as means for accomplishing that objective.

This brings me to the third role of the publisher, producing a publishable product. With all due respect to the ease with which one can use desktop publishing, I believe that creating a publishable product is not a trivial task that can be performed by clerical staff or even by the author. It involves a high level of technical expertise, experience, and knowledge of the needs of marketing and of the use of publications.

The fourth role of the publisher is marketing and distribution. This is an important role not only for the publisher, as the basis of profitability, but for the author, the users, and the libraries that will preserve the book and assure readers access to it. Evaluating the appropriate market, its size, the kind of package that will appeal to it, and the best means for informing it of availability—these are all essential, as is establishing the appropriate print run and maintaining a stock of copies for rapid delivery.

The publisher therefore fulfills critical responsibilities by controlling the process of developing the product's content, the process of production to assure quality of product, and the process of distribution to assure that the product will be available, deliverable at an appropriate price and with suitable response time.

Where are those elements of control in desktop publishing? They are missing, and the result is the likelihood, even the certainty, of degradation of quality in every respect. Of special concern is the problem of limited availability and distribution.

To highlight the various problems, let's consider desktop publishing of a scholarly journal. The tasks of reviewing and refereeing should still be there; the requirement of subscription fulfillment, with all its operational and financial complications is still there; but the maintenance of back issues becomes immensely more complicated through lack of formal procedures. From the administrative standpoint, all of this implies substantial commitments of scarce staff services, space, and facilities. It is hardly an appealing proposition.

Underlying the development of desktop publishing is the assumption, implicit in the term itself, that publishing is merely a matter of printing an acceptable product. In fact, though, production is the smallest part of the costs of publishing. The assumption will inevitably lead to disaster if the costs of marketing and distribution are ignored.

The Scholarly Aspect of Control

Let me turn now to another aspect of control, one triggered by the question of what we may encompass in terms of forms, formats, and media. Are we limiting our scope merely to printed publication? I'm sure that to do so would fail to reflect the reality of electronic publication in general, and that we need to consider the phenomenon of electronic mail.

In some disciplines, (Artificial Intelligence being a good example,) the conception is that the on-line electronic journal should replace the traditional printed page. It is more rapid, more immediate and direct, and more responsive to change. Whether that's the case or not, electronic mail is a reality of scholarly, peer group communication today. Surely it represents desktop publishing, differing only in the medium for distribution.

Another medium of desktop publication is simply the magnetic diskette. Increasingly, scholars are sending diskettes to colleagues whenever there is need to develop joint reports. In recognition of this phenomenon, the Electronic Manuscript Project of the Association of American Publishers was established to develop standards for encoding the text in such media in order to facilitate its subsequent publication.

On the horizon, if not already here, is the potential of Bernouilli boxes and optical disks, especially in the form of "write one, read many" (WORM) cartridges. We are al-

Robert M.
Hayes

ready beginning to use such forms of communication of data bases among colleagues collaborating in research and publication. I am certain that desktop publication in WORM form will similarly become a common means for distribution.

The Invisible College

From the standpoint of scholarship, the so-called invisible college clearly facilitates communication among a small peer group. But experiments with formalizing invisible colleges, undertaken some twenty to twenty-five years ago, demonstrated the improved effectiveness in communication is heavily outweighed by the inherent limitations. The peer group is by no means the only or even the most appropriate context for discussing the progress of research and for evaluating it. Research should be important beyond the limits of the peer group; it should be subject to evaluation and assessment by other minds, by other tests of validity. The cold, clear light of day needs to enter, but the invisible college, by its very mode of operation, prevents that kind of sunshine effect.

Another danger inherent in the invisible college, especially in the electronic modes of communication though less so in the printed forms of desktop publishing, is the likely loss of what I call "integrity of reference." I'd like to step aside for a moment to define that term; then I will comment on the potential dangers to it.

Scholarly communication has built up an important tradition of reference. It reflects the fact that in all areas of research—humanities, sciences, and social sciences—we progress by building on the past. And we acknowledge our debt to the past by citation to it. By doing so, we assure that our sources can be checked, verified, and validated. But that implies that referenced material must be available for checking, verifying, and validating. What happens if the source data have been erased or, worse yet, altered since they were used? The entire structure for scholarly progress would collapse. That danger is very real when we deal with electronic publication. In fact, changes in distributed databases are common, even among those that are formally published.

The Library Aspect of Control

I turn now to the issues relating to control that are the responsibility of the library. I start from the fundamental principles of the scholarly research library. There are two.

The scholarly research library, the archive, and the museum are unique among institutions in having as their societal role responsibility for preserving the record of the past. All other information industries and activities have only the objectives of immediate distribution. Publishers and communication media deal with the immediate; they take no responsibility for preserving even their own products. The film industry has ignored its own history; the video industry has erased its own programming; and the publisher ceases to have any interest (except for an almost emotional commitment to copyright protection) as soon as the book is out of print. But the library does assure that material is preserved.

The second responsibility of the scholarly research library is to provide access to the records the library preserves. The library community shares that responsibility within itself and with cognate services in the form of bibliographic utilities, secondary access tools (the indexing and abstracting services), and a variety of data base access services.

The question I must now ask is, How does desktop publishing affect these imperatives, these fundamental responsibilities? The answer is clear: there are serious problems in control of this literature. The problems which I will detail in a moment are ones with which the library field has extensive experience. They arose with the entire array of "report" literature and similar ephemera. The tools that have been developed indeed provide the means for control of such literature, but they are expensive to maintain and expensive to use. The point I want to make is that desktop publishing is merely another form of "report publication," with perhaps improved graphic and typographic quality.

The first problem in controlling desktop publishing is the lack of control of the fact of publication. With formal publishers, we have *Books in Print* and similar mechanisms

*Robert M.
Hayes*

for identifying availability and sources of materials. What will be the counterpart for desktop publications?

The second problem is the lack of means for assessment and review, so essential in making the decisions in selection and acquisition of material to be preserved. Perhaps some desktop publications will make their way into the review literature; certainly the one that I produced of the proceedings of a conference did so. But for the bulk of them, such means for assessment simply will not be available.

The third problem is the lack of means for access. There is a strong mechanism for distributing books and journals, but as yet no counterpart exists for electronic publications. If a library wished to acquire a particular desktop publication, how would it do so?

The fourth problem is the lack of the tools for secondary access—the coverage of desktop publications in the indexes, abstracts, bibliographies, and catalogs of the country. The result is that a person needing information contained in such ephemeral publications has no means for identifying those of potential value.

The final problem is that even when such material is identifiable, for example through the various citation indexes (resulting from reference to it in some formally published document covered by the citation indexes), the user has no means for establishing where to obtain it. I am reminded of a personal experience some fifteen years ago when I came across a reference to a publication that was cited by other authors. I searched in library after library, catalog after catalog trying to get access to it. Finally, I managed to track down the author of the book in which the citation occurred, visited him, and discovered that the citation was to a personal manuscript available only from him. I can visualize that experience repeated a hundredfold as desktop publishing makes it feasible to generate increasing numbers of such ephemera. The problem not only affects the users, though. From an operational standpoint, it places intolerable burdens upon librarians who must track down these citation ghosts. Do they refer to real publications? To ephemeral publications? To figments of the imagination? How is one to tell?

Summary

I have responded to the question "Who Should Control Desktop Publishing?" in ways that reflect my personal experience—as a faculty member, academic administrator, sometime publisher, researcher, and library educator. Each of these perspectives provides a different view of the issues. However, taken together my observations from these disparate vantage points do suggest that the question is a serious one, requiring joint decisions among the groups involved in information generation, distribution, preservation, and use.

Who Is in Control?

By Robert L. Oakman

My subject is the scholarly publishing of books and journals and the role of computers, especially desktop publishing, in their production and distribution. Scholarly publishing is being changed forever by computerized typesetting. With desktop publishing, an individual scholar with a personal computer, a word processor which handles alphabets in many languages, including nowadays Greek, Cyrillic, Arabic, and even Chinese characters, and a laser printer can edit and produce a journal of good quality in his or her office. The technology is there for an explosion of new journals and monographs. But will this be an unalloyed blessing? Who will control the processes of scholarly desktop publishing?

At issue it seems to me are at least the following questions. How well can desktop publishing carry out the demands of scholarly publishing? What can scholars expect to get out of it? And what can they expect to find as problems? To start with a real case, I have been helping a colleague at Bamberg University in Germany look for appropriate text-processing software and a laser printer for a bibliography of Palestinian poetry which may have German, romanized Arabic, and Hebrew text combined on the same page. Even in the old days of linotype book production, this would not have been a standard job. Because of the limited market for the bibliography, the editor had to save on production costs and therefore considered desktop publishing. Yet she did not want to sacrifice quality for cost or convenience to the reader.

Whatever program we chose had to allow shifting from one alphabet to another on the same line, and had to display all the characters from the mixed character sets on the computer screen at the same time. The resulting files needed to be produced with standard layout and formatting software for desktop publishing, perhaps directly from a laser printer. We examined several word processing systems, but some would not allow the mix-

Robert L.
Oakman

ture of fonts on the same line. Others did not provide a romanized Arabic alphabet and did not always allow the user to create new characters for personal use. We decided to use a multilingual program called the Printer Polyglot (Mikado, Berlin), available in Europe with a wide choice of alphabets and the capability for creation of new character sets. It works with WordPerfect, a standard high-quality word processing package for MS-DOS computers, and can be used with various laser printers. With the best such programs, desktop publishing can bring quality printing into scholars' offices at a price most of them can consider and with typographical features they never thought feasible.

Yet scholars are not usually people with typographical and layout experience. Leaving aside questions of quality in content, some of the scholarly work that has been produced with desktop publishing is clearly amateurish in format and appearance. My friend, Michael Farringdon, a computer scientist who has himself done some scholarly publishing of the works of Dylan Thomas, attributes the decline in quality to the fact that one cannot acquire design skills with a computer program costing several hundred dollars. A recent number of a Welsh literary magazine, created with desktop publishing, mixed up typefonts and sizes throughout the issue, flouting many typographical conventions. The result was noticeably distracting to the reader. Unlike the staffs of academic presses and publishing houses, scholar-publishers are not trained as production managers and art directors, and their results are often amateurish. Given the current overload in educational requirements for most graduate degrees, we cannot expect that scholars will be getting this kind of training in school either.

Among the custodians of the great ideas and values of the past are the scholarly editors of documents. Their editions of the diaries and works of classical authors represent a respected scholarly activity traditionally associated with quality book production.[1] Let us examine more closely how computer techniques, including desktop publishing, are being integrated in all stages of this time-honored scholarly endeavor in literature, history, and philosophy. Although the following narrative describes a hypothetical edition, the editorial practice of *The Essential Carlyle Edition*, headquartered at the University of California at Santa Cruz and being published by the University of California Press, forms the basis of much of the discussion. Let us suppose that a group of editors has completed a census of documents and decided to collect and edit the letters and journalism of a prominent thinker of nineteenth-century New England. Instead of using an index file, they store their document information in an automated filing system, which allows sorting in any number of categories and can be updated, indexed, and alphabetized at will. On a research trip to the Dartmouth Library, Professor X transcribes a cache of letters using word processing into a laptop portable machine during the day and sends the transcriptions home to his or her editorial office at night using the modem built in to the portable. A word processing system handles day-to-day editing and creation of annotation files in the editorial offices. Consulting editors regularly send each other queries and keep up with each other's progress by electronic mail systems linking their universities.

Having collected different versions of the journalism texts, including some later revised for book publication, the project has them optically read onto computer disks, perhaps by a Kurzweil scanner, a machine that bypasses keying of texts by learning to recognize different typefonts of the roman alphabet. Recent technological progress in scanning digitized images of characters suggests that the process of inputting long texts into the computer, a perennial headache of any large text project, will be less of a problem in the future than formerly. In earlier times, projects of this kind had to rely on keyboarding—relatively slow, expensive, and inevitably filled with error. The Kurzweil introduced sophisticated scanning in the early 1980s, and alternative systems are appearing every year.

The scholarly editors are concerned with noting revisions in different editions of their author's works, for they may reveal changes of mind or stylistic habit. Several collation programs that run on personal computers are avail-

Robert L. Oakman

able to collate different versions of the same article automatically from the computer files and produce sets of variants for inspection by an editor.[2] The editor then receives the texts and collations either from the central editorial office on a diskette or by modem through electronic mail. Having studied the variants, the editor amends the basic copy text and formats the table of variants before sending them back to the project office. Once the amended copy text, variant and footnote files, editor's introduction, and appendices are ready in machine-readable form, the general editor can use the computer to prepare a full scholarly index with terms and cross-references under his or her control. A number of indexing programs are available, but the CINDEX programs developed by the Henry Laurens Project of South Carolina have been found especially suitable for scholarly editions.[3] The CINDEX programs allow the scholar to choose all the index terms directly from the manuscript pages and decide on appropriate cross references. Once the CINDEX index for one volume is complete, it can be merged later with others to form a cumulative index to the multi-volume edition.

The volume is then almost ready to be sent as a computer text to the academic publisher. The editor of our edition, sitting in the project office with one of several desktop publishing programs, such as PageMaker or Ventura Publisher, can now take the machine-readable texts, try out type styles and formats on them, and get out sample proofs from the laser printer in minutes. It is not likely, however, that such a large scholarly project, which represents a sizeable investment of people, time, and money on the part of several universities and foundations, would be produced in final form in-house using desktop publishing.

About fifteen years ago, long before anyone imagined the availability of desktop publishing, Wilhelm Ott at Tübingen in Germany, a pioneer in scholarly editing with computers, began to develop a series of computer typesetting programs called TUSTEP for complex scholarly jobs. He has written extensively about special problems of text processing for scholarly editions that are not amenable to standard desktop publishing software, designed for general publishing.[4] For example, in many editions the textual notes with variants appear at the bottom of the page in smaller font than the text itself; such cases raise tricky problems of lineation and pagination in typesetting. One might think that this is a simple case of "cutting and pasting" the two texts and resizing the typefonts using the desktop publishing program. However, textual notes normally refer to a specific page and line of the text itself; yet the text cannot be properly broken up into pages and lines until the lengths of the notes themselves have been taken into account for filling out the page. Such delayed calculation of line numbers for matching text and notes is not a feature included in standard desktop publishing software.

Because of such situations, Dr. Ott argues that desktop publishing is not the solution for scholarly projects like complicated textual editions. Yet the editors will probably want to use desktop publishing to make a trial run on the computers in their offices. They can discover any great problems and test out formats and typestyles before they send off the texts, notes, appendices, and index as computer files to the publisher. Since the editors have already made the final decisions on type size, fonts, layout, and done final editing, the publisher can send out the text to a commercial typesetter and get page proofs in a few weeks. Meanwhile, copies of the desktop produced texts can be sent out by the publisher for peer review.

The whole editorial process, from scanning or keying of the original text to final proofs, has been done on one master copy of the same machine-readable file. The computer has been a part of all aspects of the scholarly project, and the traditional division of labor between scholarship and book production has been somewhat merged. Having all of this computer assistance at a central editorial office has several advantages: the editors are always in control of the work, and the press can save time and money in final editing and production. I know of at least one case in which the fact that a large scholarly edition was computer-assisted in the headquarters of the project throughout all stages of the editorial process

Robert L.
Oakman

made the edition an economically viable proposition for the academic press. With the computer as their communications device, word processor, collation assistant, storage medium, and interim printing device, the scholars did what they were trained for, the traditional roles of text editors; and the publisher provided its usual services: professional editing, layout, final typesetting, and marketing and distribution, most of them also managed by the machine. Desktop publishing served an auxiliary role in manuscript production in the editorial offices, but the final product was produced through the usual academic publishing channels.

Like typesetting with computers, new developments in the technology of computer storage with laser disks are already beginning to affect research libraries and scholarly journals and reference books. This computer storage device has the capacity to store between five hundred million and a billion characters of information on one inexpensive laser disk. To grasp the concepts of a billion characters of information, think of a general-purpose encyclopedia on one disk or a national phonebook packaged with a dictionary and *Roget's Thesaurus*— all of this information readily accessible within seconds. The encyclopedia, which sells for less than half of the bound version, can be queried to display all its references to Plato or origami, and the materials begin to scroll off the screen of a personal computer almost immediately. With the arrival of the NEXT computer, the first to use erasable optical disk memory, we can store two hundred and fifty-six million characters of information on one erasable compact disk that sells for $50. We are truly in an era where a thousand-volume library can be available for instant retrieval on a home computer.

What this technology will mean for libraries and scholarship is already becoming clear. In 1985, University Microfilms announced that *Dissertation Abstracts* was going onto laser disks and issued a call for major scholarly journals and database producers in various fields to join it in a publication partnership. Suppose five volumes of the essential journals in one field were packaged on one disk and sold to libraries and scholars. When a reader wanted a copy of an article read from the disk, the computer-monitored system would print it out and bill him or her for it on behalf of the journal. Not only would smaller libraries be able to afford a complete run of significant journals in many fields, but publishers would also be able more easily to control access to their copyrighted materials through the computer's accounting system of what had been copied. Future adaptations of this technology for access and distribution of hard-to-find scholarly materials come readily to mind. A scholar will be able to have more research materials at his or her fingertips than were stored in the great library in Alexandria.

The new frontiers in computer publishing and storage technology will have their inevitable effects—both beneficial and potentially damaging—on the conditions of scholarship, especially its preparation, reviewing criteria, and dissemination. Already a glut of scholarship inundates us all. Concern has been expressed about its quality. With high quality desktop publishing and laser disks, the quantity of the glut is likely to become greater. Departments can afford to found new journals and publish them in their offices without the need of sponsorship from academic presses. Groups of scholars can bypass the normal review processes of academic presses, which traditionally have provided academic quality control in the screening of manuscripts. Scholars can now band together in small companies and publish their research in cheaper formats than ever before. In this process, the professional editing and typesetting provided by press personnel will be bypassed. Even so, libraries will be able to archive much more information in less expensive forms and smaller space than formerly.

The technology of computers can expand enormously the quantity of scholarly research, but what of the quality? Are there aspects of the computer revolution that can affect positively the intellectual climate of research in the humanities, sciences, and social sciences of the future? The answers would seem to lie in more theoretical realms of computer science than we have been addressing here. Specifically, I would like to focus on one area in some detail: the expert system. To what ex-

Robert L. Oakman

tent may trends in this field, today not very well-known outside computer science, affect the scholarly acquisition and presentation of new knowledge?

Expert systems, a computer concept based in knowledge gathered from people about how they make decisions, may offer machine assistance in controlling the quantity and quality of scholarship. An expert system has been called "an automated copy of human expertise."[5] For a particular application, its program must contain information about how people think about the problem (its knowledge base; facts and relations among them), how they use their knowledge to make decisions (the inference engine; methods of using relations for problem solving), and how they learn from experience and adapt to changing conditions. For example, colleagues in computer science at South Carolina have been working on an expert system to teach people how to become more proficient in using the complex writing and editing routines on UNIX computers. Monitoring the user's every keystroke and function, the program decides how experienced the user is, what kind of help to offer, and when it is appropriate to give unsolicited suggestions for easier use of the machine. It also understands user questions about UNIX submitted in English and responds as an active user's manual directly at the terminal.

More ambitious is the Kurzweil Voice Report, a word processing system introduced in 1986 and upgraded in 1988 that accepts voice dictation and creates a printed document directly. In simple terms, it is an automated secretary that types out what you dictate to it. It combines multiple "expert" processors to decipher speech with a dictionary of about 5000 words and a component for understanding grammar and syntax. The system learns a speaker's frequent vocabulary, automatically adds those terms to the dictionary, and eliminates others not often used. It has built-in features to resolve ambiguities of confusing sound pairs, such as red and read or their and there. Raymond Kurzweil, the inventor of the optical scanner, plans to revolutionize the whole world with this "expert" language understanding and writing system.[6]

Given the experimental reality of the automated writing machine, we can foresee very rapid growth in the kinds of expert systems that have implications for scholarship. Automobiles and appliances already contain special-purpose microprocessor chips that serve some control function. I suggest three possible ways that analogous expert systems might be used as pre-processors to do initial screening of the quality of scholarly research. In the near future, we can expect to see programs far more comprehensive than those of today, containing a person's knowledge of grammar, usage, and meaning. Such a complex stylistic filter could check on writing with too many long, complex sentences or too many nominalized verb forms, such as we find in the language of bureaucrats. For statistical studies, another program might check an author's hypothesis to see if the statistical methods applied to it were appropriate. We have all seen studies that make statistical claims without sufficient awareness of the possible liabilities of the method. The massive memories of laser disks could store large, comprehensively cross-indexed files of back issues of all significant journals in a discipline ready for use to check the significance of scholarly work and the validity of its references.

Let us suppose that programs like these were available. Scholars could revise their work for clarity and check the appropriateness of their statistical method as they complete their drafts. Working with the machine-readable copy of a manuscript, the offices of journals and university presses could use these systems to screen submissions initially. If the article needed serious stylistic or statistical revision, the computer could notify the editors before they bother to contact outside reviewers. By checking the laser disk files cross-indexed over many volumes of many journals, the editors could decide whether an article is actually a new departure or merely a rehash of previous work. Today the impossibility of doing elaborate content searching leads to publication of similar, even repetitive research. In all these ways, expert systems could cull out articles needing revision and leave to editors and reviewers the more important tasks of deciding on work that deserves their time. The com-

Robert L. Oakman

puter would be helping scholars, editors, and publishers to keep control of the scholarly process.

I have argued that the marvelous flexibility and applicability of the computer is partially responsible for the current glut of scholarship. Word processing and desktop publishing have made writing easier, manuscripts longer, and publication simpler and cheaper, whether the ideas warrant publication or not. Several years ago, Chet Grycz, author of another chapter in this book, told me that some scholarly manuscripts appear to be three or four articles expanded to book length through the ease and convenience of word processing. With the possible assistance of expert systems, the computer itself, which has helped to foster the glut of scholarship, can help to manage it. In the hands of the right people—editors, reviewers, press staffs, and individual authors themselves—the computer can help us to promote the production of better scholarship. It can help us to present it in inexpensive and yet aesthetically pleasing format. In our role as scholars promoting the growth of our disciplines, let us not allow the ease of electronic publishing to blind us to the need for quality in the preparation and presentation of our research. Let us make sure that the message, the content of our scholarship, is at least as important as the method.

NOTES

1. For further information about the *Essential Caryle Edition*, of which the first published volume, *Heroes and Hero-Worship*, should appear in 1990, contact the Editor-in-Chief, Professor Murray Baumgarten, Kresge College, University of California, Santa Cruz, California 95064.

2. For example, there are three collation programs available for MS-DOS computers: PC-CASE (Computer Assisted Scholarly Editing), from Professor Peter Shillingsburg, English Department, Mississippi State University, MS 39762; Micro-TUSTEP (Tübingen System von Textverarbeitungsprogrammen), from Dr. Wilhelm Ott, Tübingen Universität Zentrum für Datenverarbeitung, 7400 Tübingen, Germany; and URICA (User Response Interactive Collation Assistant), from Professors Robert L. Cannon and Robert L. Oakman, Department of Computer Science, University of South Carolina, Columbia, SC 29208.

3. For an early description of CINDEX, see David Chesnutt, "Comprehensive Text Processing and the Papers of Henry Laurens," *Newsletter of the Association for Documentary Editing* 2, no. 2 (May 1980): 12-14; and 2, no. 3 (September 1980): 3-5.

4. See, especially, Wilhelm Ott, "Software Requirements for Computer-Aided Critical Editing," *Editing, Publishing and Computer Technology*, Sharon Butler and W. P. Stoneman, eds., (New York, AMS Press, 1988), pp. 81-103.

5. Bruce D'Ambrosio, "Expert Systems—Myth or Reality?" *Byte* 10, (January 1985): 282.

6. See Kurzweil's description in "The Technology of the Kurzweil Voice Writer," *Byte* (March 1986): 177-86.

The Sorcerer's Apprentice: A Publications Manager's View

By David May

The term "desktop publishing" is a dreadful distortion. Whatever phenomenon we attempt to describe by that term, two things are clear: it cannot be done on a desktop, and it certainly isn't publishing, which is defined in my dictionary as "the business or profession of the commercial production of literature...for public distribution and sale."

Despite such distortions, the term continues to gain currency because, like many other marketing terms and advertising slogans, it has a powerful simplicity. For my money, it's right up there with Chevrolet's ambiguous claim that its cars give you "more," and Gallo's assurance that one of its wines "comes in two delicious flavors, red and white."

Terms aside, however, there is no question that "desktop publishing" describes *something*, and that "something" is of great interest to many people who are convinced it will help them if they can learn how to do it. They're right on both counts. Desktop publishing is, indeed, something definite, and it is of overwhelming importance, especially to those of us who toil in the fields of university communications, publications, and printing. We need to learn what desktop publishing is, to understand why it is important, to confront the concerns it raises for our profession, and to figure out what to do about it.

What is desktop publishing?

I define it as the end product of four recent developments. The first is digital character generation. Until recently, letter forms had to be drawn by hand, cut into metal, or recorded as images on film. Now, they can be created digitally by a computer, with sufficient accuracy for us to recognize them, right on the monitor, as specific typefaces like Garamond or Baskerville or Helvetica. The second development is laser type output. Printing sharp, high quality letter forms onto a sheet of paper has been a

David May

slow and expensive process, but now laser technology has greatly speeded up the process, and thus reduced its cost. Thirdly, there is now page-layout software. Not long ago, typeset material was first printed in single columns, then arranged into pages by hand. New software programs have made it possible to computerize that once laborious and painstaking process. The last development is accessibility. The hardware and software needed to make all these good things happen are widely available, relatively cheap, and (at least compared to a linotype machine) easy to use. Although they won't actually fit onto a normal-sized desktop, they will fit into almost anyone's office or home, and, increasingly, that's exactly where they are going.

Is desktop publishing important?

You bet it is. In fact, it may well be the most revolutionary development in print technology since the invention of moveable type more than five hundred years ago.

To the layperson, desktop publishing is nothing short of magic. Ever since technology began to impose itself upon publishing in the fifteenth century, individuals who needed to "publish" something—that is, to have their words set in type and produced in multiple copies—have had to contend with a lengthy and often costly process. Further, they have had to relinquish control over their projects, at several key points in production, to those people who "owned" the technology.

Desktop publishing has eliminated all that. Now, without ever leaving their homes or offices, would-be authors can write what they wish, set it in whatever typeface they choose, lay it out to their own taste, print it out on their laser printer, and even make copies on their own copy machine. It's often faster, it's usually cheaper (or at least it seems to be), and the feeling of control is absolutely intoxicating.

To publications professionals—editors, graphic designers, and typographers—desktop publishing may be less magical, but it is no less important. In the hands of a professional, the various technological advances that comprise desktop publishing are tools of awesome power, which promise to change fundamentally the way we work.

Until now, producing a publication has been a step-by-step *linear* process, replete with duplication, repetition, speculation, and revision. It has been easy to make mistakes, and costly and time-consuming to correct them. Because text and illustrations are handled by different technologies, it has been difficult to achieve an integrated design; photographs have usually been limited to rectangular shapes inserted into the text wherever they fit.

The techniques of desktop publishing have converted that linear process into a *simultaneous* one in which all the steps occur at the same time, eliminating the duplication of effort and trial-and-error procedures that have plagued publications work for centuries, and permitting a spontaneity and flexibility of design that has been lost since illuminated manuscripts.

What concerns does desktop publishing raise?

The same kinds of concerns that would result if General Motors unleashed onto the market a jet-powered helicopter that would take off from your driveway, cut your thirty minute commute to thirty seconds, sold for the price of a Yugo, and required no license to operate.

That analogy may be a *bit* of an exaggeration, but it doesn't seem like it to those of us who manage publications and printing for academic institutions. Although our responsibilities vary with our institutions, most of us operate in three broad areas: we provide editorial, design, and typesetting services to other offices; we establish and enforce institution-wide standards of quality and consistency; and we serve as *publishers* for institutional magazines, catalogs, directories, and other materials. In all these areas, desktop publishing radically affects what we do and how we do it.

• Desktop publishing affects the kinds of skills our staff members must have, as well as the ways in which we define and organize their duties. Currently, we have staff positions for writers, editors, designers, graphic artists, typesetters, and proofreaders. We all know what those jobs are: what duties and skills they require, how they relate to one another, and what level of responsibility and reward they

The Sorcerer's Apprentice: A Publications Manager's View

David May

entail. But under the onslaught of desktop publishing technology, that clarity is disappearing as activities merge. When writing, design, and typesetting occur simultaneously on the computer screen, how will we distinguish between writers, designers, and typesetters? How will we reassign those tasks? How will we retrain staff members to do them? What will we pay them for their newly defined jobs? And what will we do with those whom we can't retrain?

• Desktop publishing affects the way we do business. Many of us, in effect, *sell* editing, design, and typesetting services to offices throughout our institutions, but, as desktop users proliferate on our campuses, our business is eroding. In many cases, we are so heavily invested in outdated technology, and so lacking in research and development budgets, that we cannot convert quickly enough to keep pace. Even if we could, I'm not sure that we *should*, because individual desktop users want the freedom to "do it" themselves. Understandably, they want access to the magic; but we fear that, like the sorcerer's apprentice, they will wreak havoc for all of us.

• Desktop publishing affects our ability to maintain standards of quality and consistency in our institution's publications. That used to be easy. Typesetting and printing technology was so arcane, so expensive, so user-hostile that individual users were forced to rely on our centralized resources. That, in turn, provided a "point of control" at which we could intercept bad writing, grammatical errors, or egregiously ugly designs that did not reflect our institutional standards. That control has now gone. With dozens of secretaries cranking out brochures, fliers, and booklets from their desks, we have no opportunity to influence what they do. Worse, we don't even know what they're doing.

• Finally, desktop publishing affects many of us personally. Few of us who manage academic publications were attracted to our jobs by illusions of wealth or power. We were attracted, rather, by our personal commitment to effective communication, accuracy, clarity, elegance—even beauty. While we recognize that desktop publishing offers us tools that we can employ to those ends, we fret about what is happening as those tools become available to others who are less trained and, frankly, less conscientious.

What should we do about desktop publishing?

For the academic publications manager, a few things are clear. We cannot oppose it, delay it, or try to contain it. That way lies disaster. On the contrary, we must be the first to embrace desktop publishing as the technology of our profession, and to gain expertise in it faster and more fully than anyone else. We must share our new expertise freely and generously. We must furnish potential users with preprogrammed disks and templates, offer them workshops and seminars, and dispatch our staff experts on "house calls" to users who need our help. We have to convince our administrations to provide us with the money and the organizational flexibility to do all this.

Finally, we must put aside our personal concerns, cultivate humility, and attain some historical perspective. To gain that, I keep reminding myself that the history of printing and publishing can be seen as a five-hundred year migration of technology into the hands of the end users.

During the Middle Ages, publishing (along with learning) was the province of the Church. Its technology was one of hand calligraphy and illumination, practiced by those in religious orders. Although printing from wooden blocks had already made some inroads, it was the invention of moveable type in the fifteenth century that transformed the technology of publishing, freed it from the Church, and placed it in the hands of scholar-printers who could supply an increasingly literate upper class with books other than religious texts.

As literacy increased during succeeding centuries, technology kept pace and continued its migration to a broader range of users. The invention of motorized presses and mechanized typesetting freed the technology for broad commercial use, and, more recently, the developments of electronic typesetting and the copy machine have made it available even to individuals.

From that perspective, desktop publishing is the final step in the migration: it places all the technology in the hands of the author and the reader, and enables publish-

The Sorcerer's Apprentice: A Publications Manager's View

David May

ing to become a direct exchange between the two of them. Inevitable as that may be, I remain concerned about it because it affects my professional responsibilities, and because I think the level of discourse will suffer.

On the other hand, I suppose there were lots of monks who felt the same way five hundred years ago.

Desktop Publishing: Its Impact on the Academic Community

By Robert J. Silverman

The old order changeth, perhaps,
but the new technologies need old-style publishing values
to prevent a chaos of babble.

There appear to be two emerging movements in higher education: a considerable percentage of faculty members will be retiring shortly, to be replaced by young scholars; and technology will play a more significant role in the everyday activity of academe. Although both events suggest discontinuities of their own—a young faculty-member cohort without the leavening, wisdom, and potted experience of the current professoriate and dramatic new approaches for producing and disseminating knowledge to students and colleagues—these changes will also influence each other in many ways. One of these is that younger academics, having experience from childhood with computer technology, are apt to use it more fully than their retiring counterparts. The use of desktop publishing in the production and dissemination of scholarship will dramatically influence how scholars create and judge research and scholarship in their fields. This chapter suggests some of the changes that are likely to occur in the publishing process as desktop publishing, defined in the broadest sense to include writing, refereeing, and distribution through the computer, and a new professoriate jointly come of age.

In general, I believe, what follows pertains to various academic fields of study and their internal differentiations.[1] Charles Bazerman notes that "the words (of a text) are shaped by the discipline—in its communally developed linguistic resources and expectations; . . . in its active procedures of reading, evaluating, and using texts. The words arise out of the activity, procedures, and rela-

Robert J. Silverman

tionships"[2] within the various communities, however one chooses to define them: in terms of their development as mature or immature fields,[3] their prominence as major or minor professions,[4] the activities of faculty who systematically develop different patterns,[5] or social and political factors both within and external to the fields.[6] Knowledge is communal: scholars belong to different discourse communities, and knowledge places them in community.[7] They develop and sustain knowledge that is appropriate for the community and attempt to influence or to make an impact on others in the context of their substantive commitments. Thus it is unlikely that desktop publishing will be used only for the private production and self-certification of scholarship. Knowledge that is not certified by one's colleagues through professionally sanctioned processes and structures is simply not knowledge, and serious scholars understand this point.

Academic work attempting to become knowledge, that is, attempting to become communal, and filtered through desktop technology leads to the electronic journal, already experimented with in Great Britain.[8] The electronic journal will be the most dramatic consequence of the spread of desktop publishing. It will foster the development of new communal patterns that at once will enrich and threaten the scholar, and will reshape the certification of knowledge and knowledge itself.

The future will likely see the combination of both the traditional and the progressive: traditional logic used by persons involved in the scholarly publishing process and new logics inherent in the technologies through which academic work flows. I believe that scholars will continue to submit their manuscripts to journals whose editors will continue to have them reviewed, though all these transmissions will be executed electronically. Existing computer programs are also more likely to be used in selecting peer reviewers and communicating with authors regarding the submission/publication process, from advice on how to prepare an article to reports on where a given manuscript is in the pipeline. Heightened systemization will allow for greater accountability and responsiveness, not insignificant benefits given the frequent complaints by authors that many editors and reviewers are less than responsive. But more important, the technology will allow journal papers to be shared on electronic networks, either on a predetermined schedule or on demand; such capability will dramatically change how we certify knowledge and, indirectly, how we certify those who are part of the process.

The most fundamental change prompted by desktop publishing—realized by electronic journals and supported by the BLEND experiment in Great Britain in the early 1980s—was increased communication accompanying the publication process.[9] In the BLEND experiment, in which the journal *Computer Human Factors* was published electronically, it was found during the course of fifteen projects that 684 hours of informal communication was shared between and among author/author, author/reader, reader/ reader in the writing and publishing process.[10] In essence, public communal review followed review for availability. Desktop publishing, then, will add another systematic layer to review. First the editor, second the reviewers, and third the field, which now will be playing a new role. Electronic journals will allow for reactions and responses to be part of the public record and allow the journal editor to have greater insight into the consequences of her or his choices and decisions regarding the specific referees reviewing a paper, to its appearance or rejection.

I expect that the role of referees will be modified from persons seeking or demanding perfection to persons judging whether a paper can enhance the conversation in the field. Referees will to a lesser extent protect a field and to a greater extent ensure quality of discourse. There are current movements in this direction, suggesting that desktop publishing will support such a development and will not challenge existing practice.

In the journal *Science and Technology Studies*, the editors in 1986 promoted the notion of "endorsing referees." After receiving referees' reports and accepting a paper, the editors wrote to referees asking them to allow their names to accompany the paper in print. The editors said, "[the] endorsement does not constitute agreement with the author's point of view or even the results of the analysis.

*Robert J.
Silverman*

Rather, it is a statement of scholarly quality, that standards of rigor and integrity have been observed in the reporting of the research."[11]

Stevan Harnad, editor of *The Behavioral and Brain Sciences*, earlier focused on the value of creative disagreement and self-correction in the advancement of fields and developed a system of open peer review to achieve these values.[12] Following the appearance of a paper that in the eyes of the reviewers can enhance conversation, a large number of peer commentators are invited to react.

Desktop publishing will allow the discourse community to consider the value and meaning of papers, thereby allowing revision following "publication." Knowledge will evolve informally through conversation as well as grow incrementally through publication. This community will probably be more demographically and geographically representative of the actual specialized community. For example, scholars from relatively poor schools will interact electronically when previously their engagement depended on spending a week in a conference city. Although technology is costly, it is becoming ubiquitous, and air fares and hotel costs will continue to be beyond the reach of many, especially younger scholars.

Although reviewers may remain anonymous (and may not publicly endorse papers), the impact of their positive recommendations will be clear to the editor and possibly the field, given the nature of the conversations that follow a paper's "availability." The quality of contributions from reviewers both before and after a paper becomes available will help editors make decisions regarding subsequent use of reviewers on the basis of such knowledge. This process might enhance the prospects for promotion and tenure of reviewers in remote locations because of contributions they make to their fields. All the "voices" might also create a great deal of noise and unprofitable engagement. As well, the changes in peer review might alter the construction of manuscripts.

In a recent book, *Science in Action*, Bruno Latour notes that an author protects his or her text against the reader's strength. A scientific article becomes more difficult to read, just as a fortress is shielded and buttressed; not for fun, but to avoid "being sacked."[13] He observes that a paper contains a "folded array of successive defense lines."[14] Clearly, effective writers have their ideal reader in mind when constructing a text, as Latour observes, and they anticipate objections in advance.[15]

Authors often attempt to promote editor's choices of peer reviewers by subtle manipulations or have a good sense of who the reviewers will be. How can one write or how will one write for the unseen enemy following the availability of one's work? Search committees and promotion and tenure committees will be more interested in the conversations following a paper than the fact of its appearance. And what if there is no conversation?[16]

But if papers are constructed differently, and one can imagine many alternatives—from less disagreement with other work whose authors might counter-attack, to more sophisticated work being submitted, to fewer papers using virtually the same data in supposedly different publications—there are likely to be changes as well in the construction of the peer review. Jonathan Potter, in a paper on reading repertoires, discusses techniques that scientists use to construct readings.[17] Because reviews are reconstructions of ideas in terms of acceptable notions and are responsive to values/norms operating in fields, electronic feedback will probably be more immediately reactive and less reconstructed.[18] To use Potter's language, will the readings be more contingent or more empiricist, that is, will reviewers focus on more personal self-interested items from the paper or the more substantive? I expect a contingent reading to be more immediate, and it may displace an empiricist version. Will the demand of the technology be such that reactions, whether contingent or empiricist, become more reactive and less leavened?

Desktop publishing has the potential of altering, through the electronic journal, how academics relate to each other and, therefore, the nature of what is called knowledge and how it evolves. The process will create greater accountability as well as greater openness, both greater defensiveness and richer engagement. The technology appears to affect the design and production of discrete products, but it is really about the way we and our

Robert J.
Silverman

knowledge commitments grow.

Desktop publishing will have dramatic consequences for those who engage with the communities they foster. I expect we will have better-managed publishing systems; we may have an increasing number of new journals established to respond to knowledge domains more widely perceived as not having a locus for dissemination; review will be systematic after as well as before publication and will be more immediate, suggesting a paper's short-term value may be overstressed; new voices will enter the review stream and more established voices will be forced out if their quality is deficient; the ethical dimension of review will be of greater importance as how we speak to each other becomes visible; authors will write more defensively; work with greater latitude may be allowed to enter the publication stream under the assumption that the field will provide the most critical reaction; how an article will be reviewed will change if one is responding to a screen image rather than a hard copy.

Impacts and the direction of impact will differ by and within fields, as suggested above, depending on existing patterns of work and by derivation on rewards, which will be reflected in promotion and tenure policies as well as practice. For example, will it be important in various fields who enters the conversation about your papers and how they do so? Will this intervention obviate the need for promotion and tenure committees to send work to one's peers when personnel actions are being considered? In an entrepreneurial age in higher education, with the resource value of knowledge a typically unspoken but very real concern, will authors' strategic and tactical sense be rewarded for its presence? (We already know that scholars of equal value gain unequal rewards because of their effective management of self.) How will younger scholars mediate the traditional norms of the professoriate with those of their turbulent technical environment, with fewer mentors available because of retirement and eager colleagues competing for tenure? Will the greater publishing effort and reflectiveness about fields change who is available to be an editor and how persons are chosen for this role? Although we may be unclear about specific impact or direction, it would be a mistake, in my judgment, to consider desktop publishing as allowing the deregulation of the academic marketplace. In fact, I believe it will reshape our discourse communities and, as a consequence, the academic communities and their practices, of which we are part.

Desktop Publishing: Its Impact on the Academic Community

*Robert J.
Silverman*

NOTES

1. See David L. Hull, *Science as a Process: An Evolutionary Account of the Social and Conceptual Development of Science* (Chicago: University of Chicago Press, 1988).

2. Charles Bazerman, *Shaping Written Knowledge: The Genre and Activity of the Experimental Article in Science* (Madison: University of Wisconsin Press, 1988), p. 47.

3. See Jerome Ravetz, *Scientific Knowledge and its Social Problems* (New York: Oxford University Press, 1971).

4. See Nathan Glazer, "The Schools of the Minor Professions," *Minerva* (July 1974).

5. See Anthony Biglan, "The Characteristics of Subject Matter in Different Academic Areas," *Journal of Applied Psychology* 57 (1973): 195-203, and "Relationships Between Subject Matter Characteristics and the Structure and Output of University Departments," *Journal of Applied Psychology* 57 (1973): 204-13.

6. See Richard Whitley, *The Intellectual and Social Organization of the Sciences* (New York: Oxford University Press, 1984).

7. See Charles Bazerman, *Shaping Written Knowledge: The Genre and Activity of the Experimental Article in Science* (Madison: University of Wisconsin Press, 1988); and Ludwik Fleck, *Genesis and Development of a Scientific Fact* (Chicago: University of Chicago Press, 1979. Originally published 1935).

8. See Priscilla Oakeshott, "The BLEND Experiment in Electronic Publishing." *Scholarly Publishing* 17 (October, 1985): 25-36.

9. See D. L. Pullinger, *BLEND-4 User-System Interaction*. Library and Information Research Report 45 (Wetherby, England: British Library Board, 1985).

10. *Ibid.*, 21.

11. *Science and Technology Studies* 4, nos. 3/4 (1986): 2. This journal of the Society for Social Studies of Science is now publishing as *Science, Technology and Human Values*.

12. See Stevan Harnad, *Peer Commentary on Peer Review: a Case Study on Scientific Quality Control* (Cambridge: Cambridge University Press, 1982).

13. Bruno Latour, *Science in Action: How to Follow Scientists and Engineers Through Society* (Cambridge, MA: Harvard University Press, 1987), p. 46.

14. *Ibid.*, p. 48.

15. *Ibid.*, p. 52.

16. Robert J. Silverman, "Author-field Interaction Following Publication in Higher Education Journals," *Higher Education* 17, no. 4 (1988): 361-75.

17. Jonathan Potter, "Reading Repertoires: A Preliminary Study of Some Techniques that Scientists Use to Construct Readings," *Science and Technology Studies* (1987).

18. Reviewers' initial reactions to papers often combine rational and affective elements that, when prepared to be transmitted to the author and editor, are recrafted to reflect rhetorical styles more in keeping with what is considered appropriate professional communication.

Issues of Access and Equity

By Deborah G. Johnson

Computers now give individuals and organizations the ability to do high quality, inexpensive desktop publishing. There is every indication that these computer capabilities will continue to improve in the future and that many more users will take advantage of them. The tough questions arise not in predicting the future of the technology or its marketability, but in comprehending the possible effects of this technology on various institutions. The focus of this chapter is on academe and in particular on issues of access and equity that may arise as desktop publishing becomes ever more available to those in academe.

A broad understanding of the social impact of computers will help us both to predict and to evaluate the impact of desktop publishing on academe. In particular, an understanding of the ways that computers change and do not change the environments they enter will be helpful.

Possibilities/Realities

Like most new technologies, computers create new possibilities for individual and for institutional behavior. James H. Moor has argued that "computer ethics" is necessary precisely because computers create new possibilities which need to be evaluated.[1] Computers, for instance, have created enormous possibilities both for assisting the handicapped and for designing more powerful and more heinous weapons systems. The task of computer ethics is to help us decide which of the many possibilities to pursue.

In the case of desktop publishing, computers have created the possibility of individuals and organizations producing and distributing huge quantities of information cheaply, with ease, and of a quality that only large and wealthy institutions could produce before. Possible uses of this new technology are mind-boggling and, depending on who uses the technology and how, the effects on academe may be for better or for worse.

*Deborah G.
Johnson*

Moor characterizes the situation when computers first enter a new environment as "a vacuum."[2] His point is that there is a vacuum in the sense that there are no laws, rules, or conventions about how to behave with regard to computers when they are first introduced. Examples of this vacuum are easy to find. When computers were first used, we had no rules with regard to privacy of electronic data, and we had no laws explicitly defining ownership rights in computer software. There was a lag time for rules and laws to develop.

On the other hand, we should remember that while there is a vacuum in the sense that Moor describes, computers are never brought into a vacuum. They are always brought into, and made use of in complex environments—environments in which there are already goals, strategies for achieving those goals, institutional arrangements, hierarchies of power, and conventions of behavior.

All of this can be said about desktop publishing in academe. When desktop publishing first became available and was brought into academe there were no rules or conventions about how it might be used, who would have access to it, or what it might be used for. Nevertheless, academe is far from a vacuum. Academic institutions have a distinct shape with goals, functions, needs, and strategies for achieving their ends. The character of academe will determine to a great extent which of the many possibilities created by desktop publishing will be pursued and how. The technology embodies many more possibilities than the narrower range of those that will be perceived and pursued.

Perhaps the most significant feature of computers is their malleability. They can be used to do innumerable tasks and in a variety of ways. It is this malleability that makes computers potentially revolutionary; that is, we think of computers as revolutionary because we see that they can transform so many of the activities previously done mechanically. However, we often fail to see that this malleability is also the very feature of computers that allows them to be nonrevolutionary. Their malleability allows computers to be used to do things the old way, to reinforce old patterns of behavior, and to prevent change.

In the 1970s as concern about the social impact of computers first gained momentum, attention centered on whether computers would cause centralization or decentralization of power.[3] The debate about this issue is relevant to access issues in desktop publishing and also illustrates the point about the nonrevolutionary potential of computers.

Initially concerns over centralization and decentralization focused on the threat to privacy created by the possibility of federal agencies maintaining huge data bases of personal information on citizens. The frightening effect of this is an increase in the centralization of governmental power. At the same time, private institutions can maintain huge data bases of information thereby increasing their power also. Some people argued that anyone high up in an organizational hierarchy would get more power from computers because that person, with the aid of a computer, could do far more on their own than ever before. In particular, individuals could manage large quantities of data without having to rely on others lower in the organizational hierarchy.[4] Not only could government agencies in Washington do more themselves without having to rely on local and state agencies; executives at the top of private corporations would be less dependent on middle managers since these top executives could handle so much more data themselves. Big businesses would use computers to become bigger and put small businesses, which could not afford or could less afford computers, out of business.Countering these arguments, many computer specialists began to argue that computers, instead of causing centralization of power, could become the great democratizer of society. The argument was easier to make as smaller, less expensive computers became available. The decentralists argued that all individuals (at home or at work) could have access to huge quantities of data. Therefore, citizens could monitor government; small business could compete with big business; and individuals at various places in a bureaucracy could know what others in the bureaucracy know.[5]

With hindsight, of course, it is easier to see that the question is much more complicated than whether com-

Deborah G. Johnson

puters cause centralization or decentralization of power. Embedded in the debate were deeper questions about the ways in which computers encourage and discourage change and whose interests computers are likely to serve.

In *Computer Power and Human Reason*, Joseph Weizenbaum used the military complex and the stock market as two examples, among others, to illustrate how computers prevent change rather than cause it.[6] He argues that these two systems were under pressure to change because the volume of activity was getting so large that the extant systems couldn't handle it. In each case a change was needed to accommodate the volume. Indeed, there was pressure to decentralize. However, computers came along just in time to allow these systems to handle the increased volume of activity and, hence, to continue in their extant form with centralized control. So, the introduction of computers prevented structural change that otherwise would have taken place.

Weizenbaum's point is further supported when one examines the ways that computer systems are designed. The process of automation involves looking at what goes on in an organization, how things are done, what the goals and priorities are, and who talks to whom in what order, and then building or buying an automated system, operated by computer, that facilitates these patterns of activities. To be sure, the shift to an automated system allows things to be done differently, and allows things to be done that could not have been done before. However, often the new possibilities are not readily perceived, at least not until later when users become more familiar with a system and its capacities. Changes that will alter the fundamental character of the organization, its ends and priorities, are not likely to get pursued. Rather, the automated system is likely to make the organization more efficient in doing what it has already been doing.

Those designing a system make decisions about who will get access to it and how. Such decisions are most likely to reflect and entrench patterns of power that already exist in an organization. Moreover, once an organization has automated its operations, there will be resistance to further change for change will now be more costly and more disruptive.

Hence, while the computerization of an activity brings about change of a certain kind, it may at the same time reinforce old patterns of behavior and old ways of doing things. This means that we should be very cautious in our predictions about what computers are likely to do in a new environment. This is especially true when it comes to patterns of access and power.

We might argue that the picture of computerization just sketched applies only to the early stages of computerization when the technology is first introduced into an environment. In these early stages the revolutionary potentials of the technology are not seen. Only after a technology has been around for awhile do we begin to see radically new ways to use it. Perhaps this is so. It would be naive and unrealistic to think that computers can counter patterns of interest and power that currently exist in organizations, be they businesses or universities, and it is these patterns that determine how computers get used and who gets access to them.

Equity and Access in Academe

Questions concerning access and equity arise when it comes to computer technology because information provides power for those who acquire it, and computers are tools for the creation and processing of information. Thus, those who have access to computers can acquire more information and distribute more information, and hence have more power, than those who do not have access to computers. When access to computers is equal, then we have equity with regard to getting and distributing information. The greater the difference in access, the greater the inequity.

Desktop publishing promises to have a more significant impact in academe than elsewhere because the mission of the university—it reason for being—is to create and transmit knowledge. The primary vehicle for this is faculty members; through teaching and publication, faculty members transmit the new knowledge they create. Desktop publishing (alone or in combination with other computer technologies) could dramatically affect the ways in which

**Deborah G.
Johnson**

faculty members publish their research. And, these new ways of publishing could affect equity among and within universities.

Faculty Publication and the Transmission of Knowledge

Recognizing a distinction between the theoretical possibilities created by computer technology and our predictions about what is likely to happen, I think it may be best to begin with some theoretical possibilities for faculty publication created by desktop publishing. Desktop publishing technology makes it possible for individuals to publish their own work in forms that are extremely easy to distribute. Depending on what is meant by desktop publishing, we can picture high quality hard copy mailed by the individual scholar, or electronic copies made readily available on-line or sent via electronic mail directly to all the scholars in the world who might be interested. These possibilities suggest a democratizing and decentralizing effect. They suggest ease of access, speed of transmission, and more control by the individual scholar. Researchers will be able to distribute their research results themselves, quickly and cheaply. Presumably such a change will facilitate the university's job of transmitting knowledge.

However, it is no small matter that the envisioned system bypasses the review process. To imagine that any system of this kind might become prominent is to fail to comprehend the importance of the review process. Faculty members are rewarded for publishing, but where they publish makes all the difference. The reward system in most universities encourages the faculty to publish in journals with peer review. The more rigorous the review system of a journal, the better it is for the faculty member to publish in that journal.

The review system serves several important functions. It testifies to the quality of the written work, hence serving the interests of those who produce knowledge. And, it serves the interests of those who use the research, for it tells these scholars that the research is worth reading. As the quantity of information available increases, scholars will be even more dependent on a mechanism to screen quality than they were before. In addition to testifying to the quality of research, the peer review system has a role in filtering out the fraudulent.

Desktop publishing makes possible a much freer, more open system, but one that cannot perform the same functions as the restricted system containing the review process. Hence, it seems unlikely that desktop publishing will altogether replace the system we now have. (Of course, there will be those who will use desktop publishing to distribute their research, bypassing the review process, but it seems unlikely that this will supplant forms of distribution that involve review, especially peer review.)

More likely, desktop publishing will change the way journals and book publishers do their business. They may well expect to receive submissions in electronic form as journals and books are made available on-line. The switch to electronic books and journals will create new problems. Given the lack of integrity of computer networks, publishers will have to deal not only with those who get access without paying, but with those who, for one reason or another, want to alter the information while it is being distributed. Publishers may not be able to guarantee the integrity of what they distribute.

More important for the purposes of this discussion, a move to electronic journals and books would raise serious equity issues. Unless every researcher has access to data lines and computers, the move to electronic publishing will do just the opposite of democratizing and decentralizing. It will reinforce and exacerbate inequities that already exist. At present, there are great inequities in resources among universities. Faculty members at the poorer universities have a much tougher time doing their research and getting it out. Inequities in access to computer technology (of any kind) follow the lines of inequities in overall resources. Students at poorer institutions have less access to computers or access only to older, less sophisticated computers. The same holds for the faculty at poorer institutions, while those at wealthy institutions have access to better, state-of-the-art equipment. These inequities will be reproduced and exacerbated with the introduction of desktop and electronic publishing.

It may be argued that these inequities will occur only during a transition period; that is, when electronic pub-

**Deborah G.
Johnson**

lishing is new, access will be unequal, but when all universities come to have some form of the technology we will have greater equity than we have ever had before. This seems highly unlikely for the reasons already given and because computer technology is likely to continue to improve rapidly so that inequity will occur in relation to who has access to the latest equipment.

Other Access Issues

Desktop publishing poses a different sort of equity problem for college and university libraries. At first glance, it appears that electronic libraries could equalize access to information as never before, for on-line data bases and electronic journals and books could mean that anyone sitting at a terminal anywhere in the world could have access to them. In this scenario, equity of access would be achieved simply by equal access to terminals. But, the critical point here is that everyone, not just some people or even most people, must have access to on-line data bases and terminals, and must be able to pay for the services provided on-line if equity is to be achieved. Well-funded electronic public libraries would contribute to equity, but not private libraries which provide data searches and information for a price.

Desktop publishing creates another sort of access issue for libraries. How are libraries to keep track of all the information that is produced and distributed? Desktop publishing makes possible production and distribution by individuals and organizations without going through any registration mechanism, e.g. the Library of Congress. It is ironic that as libraries increase their capacity to provide information, they may lose the ability to keep track of what is available.

Transmission of information is also important to universities when it comes to their own advertising. Universities now compete vigorously with one another for resources and for students, and to do so they publish information using such means as customized brochures and catalogues. Desktop publishing technology gives an advantage to those who have it. But, here again, the technology is likely to reproduce patterns of power existing long before computers. The inequity between first rank, well-endowed universities, and lower rank, poorer ones is likely to remain the same if not increase with desktop publishing.

A rather different issue has to do with access to information that universities maintain—information that others want. For example, when it comes to information about students, computers provide such information to others with speed and ease. Should others have access to this information? When students apply to and then register in a university, do they automatically waive privacy with regard to certain types of information, such as their major, their address on campus? Desktop publishing in particular and computers in general will make it easy to give access to information that perhaps should not be accessible.

Conclusion

Increasing use of desktop publishing raises serious issues of equity in academe. While the technology has the potential to democratize and equalize, there are good reasons for believing that this new technology may exacerbate extant inequities.

Deborah G.
Johnson

NOTES

1. James H. Moor, "What is Computer Ethics?" *Metaphilosophy* 6, no. 4 (October 1985): 266-275.

2. *Ibid.*

3. See Part 4, "Computers and Power" of *Ethical Issues in the Use of Computers,* Deborah G. Johnson and John W. Snapper, eds., (Belmont, CA: Wadsworth Publishing Company, 1985).

4. See Abbe Mowshowitz, *The Conquest of Will: Information Processing in Human Affairs* (Reading, MA: Addison-Wesley Publishing Company, 1976); and Herbert A. Simon, "The Consequences of Computers for Centralization and Decentralization," in Michael L. Dertouzos and Joel Moses, eds., *The Computer Age: A Twenty-Year View* (Cambridge, MA: MIT Press, 1979).

5. See, for examples, H. Sackman and B.W. Boehm, eds., *Planning Community Information Utilities* (Montvale, NJ: AFIPS Press, 1972); and Rob Kling, "Computers and Social Power," *Computers & Society* 5, no.3, (Fall 1974): 6-11.

6. Joseph Weizenbaum, *Computer Power and Human Reason: From Judgement to Calculation* (San Francisco, CA: W. H. Freeman, 1976).

On The Proper Role of Desktop Publishing in the Environment of Scholarly Publishing

By Czeslaw Jan Grycz

There's no denying that the capabilities available today in even the least expensive desktop publishing software packages are *extremely* useful in the hands of knowledgeable users. The application of such programs in appropriate situations can save considerable time and money. Accordingly, they have been the focus of intense interest by scholars and their academic publishers.

As a publishing professional, I can attest to the advantages of computerized desktop publishing programs over their mechanical paste-up and assembly counterparts. Comparative "what if" scenarios, providing immediate alternative viewpoints, can be rapidly played out on a screen to augment publishing or design decisions. Attempting to do the same in a mechanical mode would be tedious and time-consuming. Those who employ desktop publishing programs can—from the same computer—participate in workgroup or national communications networks. A variety of peripheral devices can be attached to workstations, providing a wide range of output possibilities, both in-house and through service bureaus. The easy availability of spreadsheet and database programs, so integral to the day-to-day publishing business, and a wide variety of editorial and style checkers, thesauruses, and specialized dictionaries provide functionality of high value. Sophisticated laser typography provides a printed result, locally and inexpensively, that competes both in quality and price with high quality typesetting from external vendors. In other words, a variety of diverse capabilities in the machines can be used for desktop publishing, while the programs, themselves, consolidate several traditionally distinct functions.

Many publishers have established desktop publishing

Czeslaw Jan Grycz

units, confident of the advantages of improved copy control, reduced expenses for conventional typesetting, availability of last-minute copy correction, and condensed processing time. Most implementations, thus far, appear to be in marketing departments, where direct and immediate cost-benefits may be obtained for catalogs, direct-mail brochures, point-of-purchase displays, and personalized mail promotions.

A growing number of publishers are simultaneously experimenting with the preparation of camera-ready copy for books, even though the quality standards and volume output requirements for books are considerably more demanding than they are for shorter or more ephemeral documents. (Pages are said to be camera ready when a master has been assembled, since replication in quantity generally depends on photographing an original master page. The resulting negative is then used to expose a printing plate, from which a printer can ultimately reproduce as many copies as may be required.)

The Pressure to Computerize

Institutions are inherently conservative. Hence, it is not surprising that the greatest pressure on scholarly publishers to use computers results not from their own conviction that computerizing can reduce costs or enhance controls, but from the enthusiasm of individual authors. Authors are frequently puzzled and disappointed to learn that the publishing organization with whom they work is not as enthusiastic as they about enhanced electronic processing of manuscripts. Part of the authors' enthusiasm may be due to an infatuation with the ability to compose and lay out actual designed and printed pages. This selfsame ability is seen as counter-productive by the publisher who wishes to contribute editorial and structural values to a submitted manuscript. A pre-formatted manuscript may interfere with a publisher's ability to introduce changes easily.

Because so much functionality can be placed on the user's desk, it is easy for an *author* to identify real dollar savings over conventional methods of manuscript preparation. Add personal productivity enhancements, and it is difficult for an *author* not to justify acquiring a computer on the grounds that it will surely prove of inestimable worth. While this is self-evident to the individual author, there is no justification for extrapolating its truth to the larger publication process.

The Distinction Between Commercial and Scholarly Publishing Applications

J
ust a few years ago, Steven Jobs, co-founder of Apple Computer, predicted that desktop publishing would soon be built-in to all competitive computer systems, since everyone would use desktop publishing to enhance the presentation of marketing or business information. His position is understandable, since much recent growth of the computer industry depends on the premise that desktop publishing is essential to contemporary business communication. For business scenarios, he may well be correct. In the specific circumstance of *scholarly communication*, however, the very capabilities provided by sophisticated desktop publishing software may detract from an author's attention to the time-honored responsibilities of accuracy, verification, and objectivity. None of these has much to do with the *form* given to a particular document.

The skills required for desktop publishing include experience specific to editorial clarity, aesthetics, book design principles, and typesetting conventions with which few scholarly authors are familiar. As a result, we can conclude that a prodigious waste of resources and time has already taken place, involving many faculty researchers who have attempted to acquire relatively arcane skills, secondary to their primary area of study. This is true also for publications officers who have accommodated to well-intentioned but frequently inferior work. By coercing inexpertly prepared electronic manuscripts into a common mold, they have focused their attention on solving complicated technological problems, rather than on enhancing the quality of the manuscript for which they are responsible.

On The Proper Role of Desktop Publishing in the Environment of Scholarly Publishing

Czeslaw Jan Grycz

The Role of Technology in Publishing

No doubt like most of us, the stirrings of my intellectual life were prompted by hearing bedtime stories and fables read from books. The mental evolution I have enjoyed since those imaginative evenings is inextricably bound to books, or connected to impassioned conversations based on information I have read. As a result, I find it hard to overestimate the efficacy of books, their ability to legitimize and communicate scholarly research. This may lead some to conclude that there is no alternative to books for communicating scholarly information. Clearly, such an opinion is narrow-sighted. For some of today's electronic and digital resources, combining as they do text, graphics, animation, color, and sound, foreshadow an efflorescence of publishing and pedagogical opportunity. Technology will have an important impact on the evolution of scholarly communication. Where it is likely to have its greatest impact, however, is in expanding the potential of the existing publishing *system*. Desktop publishing, as a program application, deals with but one output option. As such, it does not enhance the publication *process*, but merely automates an output *result*.

A System View of Scholarly Communication

Turning our attention to the publication process is a valuable exercise. Among the prominent and perhaps unexpected contributions credited to books is the organizational structure and publishing method that has arisen to support creation of the physical artifact itself. This structure and these procedures are too little understood by those who market desktop publishing software. As a result, the achievements and capabilities they claim for their software are far greater than they could possibly encompass. This is largely because marketing strategists do not differentiate between business and scholarly applications. The scholarly communications market is too small to merit individualized advertising which might clarify the ambiguities that result from copy that promotes software for business applications only. Since those who market desktop publishing software do not distinguish between business and scholarly applications, it is especially important for us to be discerning about the proper applicability of programs for scholarly use.

As a system, scholarly publishing depends on the collaboration of *many* people, each of whom contributes a specialized skill. The role of each contributor has evolved over time to serve the needs of the academic community. An initial, tentative contact with an author gradually changes to a dialogue between that author and an editor. Such dialogue has to be collegial, supportive, and sufficiently distant from the commercial aspects of the business so as not to get entangled and distracted by them. The ability to conduct this dialogue defines the kind of person and the skills required in a sponsoring or acquisitions editor.

In many cases, the dialogue between an author and an editor results in the submission of a draft manuscript. The draft is circulated among the author's colleagues in an anonymous review procedure intended to objectify the critique of the work. After incorporating suggestions or defending his or her position, the author submits a revised copy to the copy editor whose turn it is, then, to review the work dispassionately, often suggesting changes in the very organization of the manuscript, refining an author's style, and contributing professional skills of consistency, proofreading, and indexing to it. Following that, or, more often, contemporaneously with it, the designer becomes involved, coaxing sometimes arcane material into visually pleasing form; couching the author's meaning in an appropriate aesthetic. The designer's effectiveness in accomplishing this results from a wide range of practical experience with legibility and readability of manuscripts.

The production and manufacture of the book is no less carefully attended to by largely unnoticed craftsmen and women in industrial plants. Their contribution to the finished book is essential. *All* these functions are supervised by another specialist, the publisher, whose responsibility for the fiscal viability of a list of titles ensures that a balance is maintained between miserliness and excess in the execution and presentation of a book. When books arrive in warehouses the marketing and distribution staff take over to announce the books to their widest audience. The

On The Proper Role of Desktop Publishing in the Environment of Scholarly Publishing

*Czeslaw Jan
Grycz*

staff seeks to deliver them promptly.

Chief among those who provide long-term access to the work are the librarians into whose custody we commit so many of our specialized monographs. In addition to these more or less familiar functions are countless external participants: typesetters, printers, binders, reviewers, wholesalers, jobbers, and book store managers, each of whom plays a role in the publication process.

Even so casual a review of the book publication process as I've just given shows that publishing a book is a *process* not an *event*. Such a process depends both on collegiality and specialization. It has evolved out of years of interaction between authors and publishers. We should take note of both its interrelatedness and its separate parts.

The Structure That Has Evolved in Support of Book Publishing Must be Adapted to New Technology

The university's organizational structure is currently immature with respect to new techniques of communication using the technology of computers. Because some units of the university have become more closely interrelated through the use of computers, their relationship to one another is no longer clear. On most campuses, there is an ambiguity of roles and responsibilities between the computer center and the library, for example, or between various centralized publications offices and more remote faculty research institutes. We know that such relationships are undergoing change. We can feel its effect. We need to clarify some of the issues, but we don't yet possess many collective skills in managing *change* itself. This skill is necessary because of the rapidity of technological evolution. Because social adaptation is slower than technological change, people often feel obliged to defend their territory when a new technology is introduced that threatens it. Clearly, new amalgamations and collaborations will need to be formed. For example, pressures, both negative in terms of the economics of higher educational institutions, and positive in terms of the promise of creatively applied resources for new technology, are forcing us to develop new collaborations among the resource providers on our campuses. In the meantime, however, the absence of suitable guidelines causes mixed results.

The proliferation of computers and their application to traditional academic and business activities can scarcely be overstated. Computers entered our consciousness abruptly. Their appearance, and our rapid addiction to them, has been explosive. First introduced as innocuous tools designed to help us perform our work, computers have taken over our lives, demanding as much attention as we can devote, eating up our time at an astonishing rate, and requiring considerable training. Shoshana Zuboff, in her excellent analysis of the impact of computerization on labor, suggests that these changes are far more than superficial.[1] We have been seduced by computers' abilities and their nanosecond instantaneous gratification. We are comforted that the lack of discipline in our thinking is compensated for by the fact that "It is so easy to correct one's drafts." We have become garrulous rather than precise: "It is so easy to write more." We are distracted from the costs associated with such seduction: "If I can do it all myself, it *must* cost less."

What is the impact of all this on academic life? Make no mistake: computers have already become the *sine qua non* of academic life. In a few years, computers have become essential for word processing and text preparation; number crunching and mathematical analyses; drawing, drafting, and graphics; communication and telecommunication; database assembly and retrieval; workgroup and national networking; and hypertext and linking techniques among disparate sources of information. Pedagogical applications and computer-aided instructional systems already coexist with traditional educational tools in our kindergartens and grammar schools. Medical, professional, and scientific schools clearly depend on them to cope with the burgeoning volume of scientific data. Library uses of computers for record access and networking are so great that expenses for software and hardware frequently outstrip expenses for the acquisition of the books we originally created the libraries to collect and organize. The use of computer databases for administration provides perhaps the *only* means of controlling and enumerating the activities of our student and staff populations.

Over the horizon, there looms a proliferation of mass

On The Proper Role of Desktop Publishing in the Environment of Scholarly Publishing

*Czeslaw Jan
Grycz*

storage devices, expert systems, artificial intelligence applications, which are, simultaneously, a solution and an ongoing challenge. The *solution* is contained in their marvelous capabilities. The *challenge* is in our ability to integrate established values with new technological tools.

As can be seen from the above description, publication is fundamentally a *process*. Computer applications, on the other hand, generally deal with somewhat more superficial—albeit tedious—individual *activities*.

How is Desktop Publishing Different?

A growing number of academics may be heard to complain that the freedom they expected from computer technology has turned out to be ephemeral. Some claim, somewhat paradoxically, that their word processors constrict them to less intellectual work by forcing their attention to an unfamiliar level of detail. Certainly those who attempt to become expert using simple desktop publishing programs, soon find themselves in a forest of unfamiliar acronyms, functions, and terminology. Contrary to received advertising wisdom, computers do not always make scholarly work any easier; indeed, for a while, they make things far more difficult.

As a computer application, desktop publishing is the first integrated application that rather determinedly challenges the *process* of publication by potentially circumventing the role of peer review and confusing the contribution of editors, designers, and publishers. It offers to merge these traditional functions in one software program that can generate attractive pages. Because such pages are under the author's control, advertisers suggest that desktop publishing provides a nirvana of instantaneous gratification, precisely in the area where academics feel greatest vulnerability, publication.

But the real work of scholarship, and the serious work of publishing, is, at its core, methodical and challenging, and depends almost exclusively on the liveliness of mind, not the nanosecond speed of a silicon chip. Research is an engrossing task. It is too bad that budget constraints make us vulnerable to suggestions that by doing things ourselves, eliminating the middle-man or woman, we scholarly authors can save time and money, and retain greater control over our publishable work. Because there is scant evidence, in our particular milieu, that this is so. The evidence, in fact, points to the opposite conclusion. In spite of examples touted by computer and software firms to demonstrate the democratic and salutary influence of desktop publishing, few individuals can harness the requisite skills for both sound research and aesthetic presentation.

On The Proper Role of Desktop Publishing in the Environment of Scholarly Publishing

Valid Assumptions?

Is it really a scholar's nirvana to have one's latest thought published at the moment of its birth? Is it possible for an individual to replicate a community of individuals through some form of expert system on his or her computer, and gain the same benefits of objectivity, conversation, and critique as those upon which scholarly exchange presently depends? Is it cost-effective for a specialist in an academic discipline to engage in the complicated process of evaluating one desktop program's suitability over another? And once the specialist has chosen a program, is it appropriate for him or her to devote hours to training in order to become familiar with it and to realize—in the doing—that there is a whole cultural inheritance of aesthetic judgments, terminology, and practical experience that one should understand? If the contemporary Renaissance scholar is able to do all that, and still keep current with the literature in his or her field, is there any guarantee that a book so published, or launched on the ether networks, will find its suitable audience?

Challenges of the Future

To change the perspective slightly, there are some fourteen thousand publishers listed in the current edition of *Books in Print.* The anticipated proliferation of self-publishers may shoot that figure into the stratosphere. How will we, as a society of scholars, (since it is already difficult to do so now,) find our way through such a bibliographic morass, to identify those articles or books worth our attention?

The answer to this is that the imprint of existing scholarly publishers will continue to be essential, and will serve

Czeslaw Jan Grycz

increasingly as a valuable sign of credibility and legitimacy. Even if we allow that the *range* of imprint possibilities will expand in an electronic environment, we must nevertheless conclude that the system we have established for reviewed publication is worth preserving. For electronics to serve us as well as has cellulose, we must devote attention to handselling it. This means self-reflection, and evaluation of the roles, functions, and interrelationships of all parties within the system. This focus is far different from the currently engrossing ones of software functionality, platform preferences, performance benchmarks, and user interfaces.

Authors' ultimate responsibility

What, after all, is the responsibility of authors in preparing texts for publication on their computer? It is what it has always been: to provide an editor with the most lucid theses in the most flexible *un*formatted form. This conclusion challenges the premise by which desktop publishing systems are marketed. Their principal attraction is the ability they provide to format pages, but publishers, in fact, seldom want their authors to submit print-like manuscripts. The appearance of a print-like manuscript obscures the state of its preparedness. And a manuscript already formatted in pages usually necessitates a great deal of undoing of the formatting, especially if editorial attention is required, or the most appropriate page size for the book happens to differ from the author's. Publishers have, over time, established a common submissions policy and virtually every word processing program in use can provide it: double-spaced lines on 8-1/2 x 11 stock, in a typewriter-like font that supports romance language diacritics, printed with sufficiently wide margins for annotation.

Structured Tagging

In the future, it will become increasingly useful to receive electronic versions of the same document, unformatted, but structurally tagged, enabling computer identification of all the elements in a text. A practical application depends on the universal transferability of files from one computer system to another. ASCII performs this function for character sets. Until recently, there was no satisfactory way of communicating sophisticated information about the *structure* of a manuscript, or its various levels of emphasis.

The Association of American Publishers, in conjunction with a wide-ranging list of scholarly bodies has established a comprehensive document description for book tags, in which the description is based on a standard, called SGML (Standard Generalized Markup Language). SGML is rapidly finding its way into software programs and desktop publishing workstations. The federal government, through its CALS initiative, mandated that by 1990 all government contractors had to be in compliance with this standard. This spurred manufacturers and software developers to integrate the standard into their products, which may be a boon for publishers. In the academic world, already, University Microfilms International, which is the repository in Ann Arbor, Michigan, for theses and dissertations, has announced it will accept a manuscript on any diskette or magnetic medium, if it complies with the SGML standard. Such acceptance will be made in lieu of the obligation for "5 copies on 100% rag bond, typewritten with a new typewriter ribbon, etc." As important, a broad-based coalition of scholarly organizations, under the guidance of the "Text Encoding Initiative," is formulating a set of tagging conventions, suitable for actual scholarly texts and use.

On The Proper Role of Desktop Publishing in the Environment of Scholarly Publishing

The Advantages of Adopting Tagging Standards

There are many implications for us in endorsing such standards, and in providing the training in our institutions for their implementation. Presently we have *no* assurance that a document prepared on a desktop publishing system in 1990 will be readable by a machine performing the same functions in, say, 1993. A file prepared according to a standard ought to be archivally more permanent. The probability becomes higher that new equipment will conform to a standard, lessening the possibility of obsolescence. We may expect that future generations of equipment, conforming to standards, will permit access to prepared texts, even if their visual, audio, color, or operat-

Czeslaw Jan Grycz

ing implementations are considerably more advanced than present versions. It is also foreseeable that library networks in the near future will carry an increasing amount of electronic data. Standards are not isolated concerns; they affect the efficiency of the entire spectrum of contributors to scholarly exchange.

The assurance that material submitted for publication will come to publications departments and academic publishers in predictable and fairly consistent manner has *operational* advantages as well. It will permit publications units on our campuses to invest more confidently in equipment and staff training if they know there is a standard to which future acquisitions will conform. Currently, the rapidly changing software and hardware environments preclude effective long-range planning. Equipment investment is difficult to justify, since there are so many competing and mutually exclusive systems in use. A universal standard obviates the need to chase after the newest entrant into an already crowded hardware/software field. It allows the publishing specialists to decide when it is appropriate to use high quality typesetting, or when it is preferable to produce laser output for a particular audience. It permits consideration of electronic distribution of certain narrowly focused manuscripts, as one of several output options, including print.

Conclusion

I suggest, in conclusion, that in its present iteration desktop publishing is essentially a *professional* tool, most effective in the hands of *trained publishing professionals.* I take the somewhat unpopular position that authors should refrain from involvement with desktop publishing except in those specialized applications where their labor will be cost-effective in preserving or opening a particular disciplinary need.

I am not bold enough to believe that what I have suggested in this chapter will find uniform acceptance. Those who advocate the widespread dissemination of desktop publishing systems among faculty enjoy enthusiastic support from those who may have been stymied by the rigor, politics, or inefficiencies of traditional publishing outlets.

The popularity of desktop publishing is an indication of just how attractive it is for an author to integrate *content* and *form*. Perhaps its very popularity will force change in what is too frequently described as an antagonistic relationship between author and editor.

My comments are intended to promote a critical dialogue on the topic, in the hope that we might publicly debate and better understand the roles of author, editor, publications manager, librarian, and university administration with respect to publishing itself, and desktop publishing in particular. The sooner we do so, the sooner will we be able to deal with the more significant issues of *nonprint* dissemination of scholarship. These are far more important considerations than those which surround the relatively narrow concerns about which person most appropriately creates pages or camera-ready copy.

On The Proper Role of Desktop Publishing in the Environment of Scholarly Publishing

NOTES

1. See Shoshana Zuboff, *In the Age of the Smart Machine* (New York: Basic Books, 1988).

Cutting Costs

By Charles L. Creesy

Princeton University Press would not have gone into desktop publishing if it were not less expensive than conventional typesetting. In this chapter, I will offer Princeton University Press as a case study demonstrating that it is possible to save money—as well as shorten production schedules and gain quality control—by doing page composition on microcomputers.

This is not to deny that without careful planning, proper training, and sound management it is possible to lose money at desktop publishing—as at any other enterprise. As Susan Gubernat, editor of *Publish!* pointed out in 1989 at a conference on "The Impact of Desktop Publishing on University Life," efficient use of the technology depends on carefully matching the right tools to the right jobs.[1] Moreover, stated savings depend on one's accounting assumptions, and may not include all hidden costs or allow for the fact that those who go into desktop publishing have to take on some tasks that printers used to do for them (at a price). In calculating desktop publishing costs at Princeton University Press, we amortize hardware and software expenditures over five years and charge them to specific jobs at an hourly rate, along with labor and overhead. Though there is an allowance for down time, capital costs are somewhat understated because the systems are not in use every working hour. But, since capital costs are less than 10 percent of the labor cost of operating these systems, this does not skew the accounting significantly. Comparisons are then made to what it would cost to do the same work at our own printing plant or at outside type houses.

Magazine Production

The first publication at Princeton University Press to go to desktop publishing was the *Princeton Alumni Weekly,* which runs about 600 editorial pages a year (exclusive of covers and advertisements). The magazine had already worked out a system whereby all editorial matter was

Charles L. Creesy

saved on floppy disk and coded so that galleys could be produced on the printing plant's Penta typesetting system without rekeying. Two sets of galleys were supplied to the editorial offices: one would be marked up with editorial corrections and the other would be waxed and positioned on page dummies to indicate the desired layout. These would be returned to the printing plant, where the corrections were keyed into the Penta, final galleys were printed out on a Linotron 202, and paste-up artists would follow the instructions on the dummies to produce precision camera-ready "mechanicals" of the pages. Photocopies of the pages were then sent back to the editorial offices and were marked up with further corrections. If these were not too extensive, just the corrections would be entered into the Penta, printed out, and "stripped" onto the flats. If they were so extensive as to make stripping impractical, the entire galley would be rerun and replaced on the mechanicals.

With desktop publishing, the floppy disk that goes to the plant and is run through the Linotron 202 contains instructions for printing finished pages instead of galleys. All the earlier galley and page corrections have been made in the editorial offices and proofed on laser output. The labor that goes into designing the layouts is theoretically no greater with computerized page composition than it was when done manually, though the ease of making changes may tempt the designer into tinkering longer. The duplicate effort of the paste-up artist at the printing plant ($30 per hour with overhead) is largely eliminated, except for overlays and minor touch-up. Use of the Penta is entirely circumvented, and the amount of photographic paper going through the Linotron 202 is reduced 80 percent or more. The main shift of workload from printing plant to editorial office is the manual entering of corrections into the computer, which is now being done by more highly paid employees than formerly. There is an editorial gain here, however, since the corrections can be made more quickly and the result immediately seen on screen and altered if necessary (avoiding additional correction cycles). In other words, the trade-off for a little extra work is greatly increased control over the final product.

When all the numbers are added and subtracted, the annual savings that desktop publishing is bringing to the *Princeton Alumni Weekly* is somewhere between $20,000 and $30,000. To keep things in perspective, this amount is not very much compared to the $500,000 or so a year that the magazine pays for printing, paper, and postage, but it still exceeds the cost of a high-end desktop publishing system.

Marketing Applications

Princeton University Press has realized its greatest cost savings from desktop publishing in the marketing department, which now produces all of its materials—seasonal and discipline catalogs, advertisements and direct-mail pieces, order forms and exhibit posters, even a complete list of books in (and out of) print—on desktop systems using a Varityper VT-600 for final output. This laser printer provides four times the resolution of a standard 300-dpi machine, high enough to make the "jaggies" disappear, at a cost of 50 cents to $1 a page. All marketing copy is written and edited on word processors and moved in electronic form from one stage to the next and from one project to another: for example, from jacket copy to seasonal catalog to discipline catalog to advertisements for various journals.

Besides saving the marketing department between $40,000 and $60,000 annually, the new technology has enabled its direct mail operation to produce special promotional pieces for individual books that it simply didn't have the time or resources to do before. A flyer can be adapted from catalog and advertising copy, composed on a desktop system, output on a laser printer, "printed" on a photocopy machine, addressed and mailed—all in a few hours. The ultimate result is a revenue gain from increased sales rather than a cost savings, but the bottom-line impact is the same.

With roughly a dozen employees involved in various capacities, the marketing department constitutes Princeton University Press's largest single application of desktop publishing. The department also requires the most technical support. The press has two in-house computer specialists whose job is to keep all the hardware running, shop

Charles L.
Creesy

for supplies and equipment (a lot of money can be saved by careful bargain hunting), train personnel how to operate the programs, rescue them when they get in trouble, keep current on technical developments, and advise staff members of new software that might prove useful. This kind of resource is essential if nontechnical people are to make efficient use of the technology. With computer equipment Murphy's Law reigns supreme: anything that can go wrong, will go wrong. Having staff members available at all times to perform rescue missions eliminates what would otherwise be countless hours wasted by employees struggling with hardware or software problems. In addition, these specialists run frequent training courses and give individual coaching to make users more productive.

While having this kind of support obviously pays big dividends, it requires a fairly large number of users to be cost-effective. Most universities have central resources to help meet these needs, but desktop publishing may pose special challenges beyond the competence of a general-purpose technical staff. In any event, given the "hidden costs" of setting up systems, training personnel, and providing ongoing technical support, an organization needs to attain a certain volume of work before desktop publishing can realize its full cost-saving potential.

Book Production

Of the twenty or more books that Princeton University Press had completed or had in production using desktop page composition as of early 1990, more were selected for that process of composition in order to speed production than to minimize costs. While it is still too early to quantify the results precisely, the desktop projects appear to be running from 30 to 45 percent below the press's target rate of eleven dollars per page for conventional typesetting (including camera-ready copy from the Linotron 202). A few books now in production will be output on the Varityper VT-600, making possible a total composition cost of less than four dollars per page. Cost reductions of that magnitude make it economically feasible to publish books with low sales potential and correspondingly low print

Desktop page composition is most efficient when not only the original copy or manuscript is received in electronic form but also all successive processing or editing is performed on screen. If one is dealing with a large number of outside authors using a wide variety of word processors and brands of computers, it is helpful to have someone on staff become expert in disk conversion. Just as important as capturing initial keystrokes is translating the internal coding of the author's word processor into coding that one's desktop publishing software can understand, so as to preserve special instructions such as italics and superscripts. The skill with which this is done will determine how much or how little hand coding is required, with obvious implications for potential cost savings.

Princeton University Press's experience accords with the conventional wisdom that up to 30 percent of composition costs can be saved by using an author's word processor files instead of rekeying a manuscript. If copy editing is done on screen, a certain amount of coding can become an automatic, almost unconscious, part of the editing process, and even higher savings are possible. If editing is done on hard copy, then there will be the added expense of transferring corrections to computer files and less money will be saved. When manuscripts are not available in electronic form, optical scanners can be used to convert them to computer code. A high degree of accuracy—we have come to invoke the Ivory Soap standard of at least 99.44 percent pure—is necessary for this to be practical. Since format codes will have to be entered by hand after scanning, the process is most efficient when it can be combined with copyediting on screen.

Division of Labor

Princeton University Press's marketing and book operations have taken different approaches toward defining the roles of personnel involved in desktop publishing projects. The marketing department has experienced the blending and overlapping of functions that is so often encountered in desktop publishing. Copywriters have become concerned with line breaks and other design questions, while the designers have become more involved in

Charles L. Creesy

production matters and occasionally have to enter corrections into text files. On the book-production side, in contrast, a new division was created with specialists trained to run the in-house page composition systems. The thinking was that editors should continue to edit and designers should continue to design and not get more involved in typesetting.

The reasons for these differing approaches arise from the nature of the work. In marketing, copy is often written (or rewritten or adapted) to fit pre-designed specifications, and on many projects there is considerable interaction between copywriter and designer as teams work to meet rigid deadlines. In the case of special promotional pieces for individual books, generally the text is adapted and the design created by one person. With books, on the other hand, the design is created to accommodate the text—which was written by an outside author. The various functions of each person are more specialized, and the pace is usually more measured. Thus it is more efficient for each participant to stick to that part of the job he or she knows best. Nonetheless, a great advantage of doing books in-house with desktop publishing is the ease of consultation among editor, designer, and composition specialist throughout the production process.

The exception to the rule is heavily illustrated and design-intensive books. In these cases, as in magazine work, having the designer do the page composition eliminates what would otherwise be an expensive, as well as a time-consuming, cycle of corrections—and shipments back and forth between editorial office and printing plant—if they were laid out by conventional means. Since the designer needs to be involved on a page-by-page basis, doing the layout on computer also eliminates what would be essentially a duplication of effort by paste-up personnel. Moreover, combining paste-up with page composition gives the designer much greater control over the final product.

To sum up, I hope the foregoing is persuasive that significant cost savings are realizable with desktop publishing. These savings should be more than sufficient to cover the capital expense of the necessary hardware and software as well as the shift of workload from printer to editorial office.

To be sure, page composition does not account for a very large part of total publishing expenses; only so much can be squeezed out of the pre-press component. But it becomes a relatively larger factor when print runs are low, as is the case with much specialized scholarly publishing. And while cost containment is only one benefit of desktop publishing—the gains in production speed and quality control may well be more important—it is the one that makes the others possible at a time of tightening resources in academe. If we don't attempt to take advantage of the cost-saving potential of this technology, and at least make it pay for itself, we run the risk of losing its other benefits as well.

NOTES

1. Susan Gubernat, "Editing and Quality Control." Presentation at "The Impact of Desktop Publishing on University Life," cosponsored by Syracuse University and the Association of American University Presses, Syracuse, NY, March 13-14, 1989.

In Pursuit of Improved Scholarly Communications

By Robin P. Peek and Joan N. Burstyn

No other institution than academia has made publishing the basis of its rewards as well as its communication process. The scholarly journal is unique. It serves both as a touchstone for promotion and tenure decisions and as a forum for new scholarship. It is, however, expensive to maintain, not only for those who publish journals but for those who form the backbone of its financial support, the academic libraries.

Though the problems of scholarly communication have been long noted, the discussion has become especially heated in the past five years. Both scholars and librarians complain that academic journals are "audaciously overpriced, always late, budgetarily and bibliographically out-of-control, technologically vestigial, and overabundant."[1] Some suggest new information-storage technologies and publishing techniques, such as CD-ROM or electronic publishing, to conquer the serial problem in academic libraries and improve scholarly communication.

This chapter explores the history of scholarly journals and the recent attempts to change their nature through electronic publishing. Our intention is to show that to publish scholarly work electronically is more complex than the literature would indicate.

Currently, authors disagree on the definition of an electronic journal. In this chapter we adopt Anne B. Piternick's definition. Piternick distinguishes between an electronic journal, which "requires that all the material be produced and stored only in electronic form," and an on-line journal, which may be accessed electronically but is also available in print.[2]

A Brief History of Scholarly Communication Practices

Despite the many years that the scholarly journal has existed, it has defied consistent definition. Journal articles (or papers) evolved from private letters. Prior to the journal, "each scholar wrote to his fellows and replied

*Robin P. Peek
and Joan N.
Burstyn*

to those who wrote to him."[3] The earliest journal that has survived, *Philosophical Transactions of the Royal Society of London*, began publication in 1665 in response to a desire for wider distribution and more timely release of scientific information.[4] According to Derek de Solla Price, the journal was to serve as a digest of "books and doings of the learned all over Europe."[5] By 1699, twenty scholarly journals were being published in Europe.

During the following two centuries there was a steady increase in journals in Europe, and then in the United States and other industrializing nations, reflecting the evolution of professions and the expansion of colleges and universities. In the United States, early in the twentieth century, the growth of specialized academic fields of research led to a proliferation of journals, primarily generated by professional organizations and university presses.

The format of the journal article also has a long tradition, originating from the length of papers delivered orally at meetings of scholarly societies. A scholarly journal usually contains several papers, each reporting work that has taken a scholar several weeks or months to complete.[6] Such papers have remained the keystone of scholarly publishing despite long-standing criticisms and attempts to provide alternative formats. As John Ziman has noted: "The invention of a mechanism for the systematic publication of fragments of scientific knowledge may well have been the key event in the history of modern science."[7]

A shift in the ownership of journals occurred in the United States after World War II, when increased funds for medicine, science, and technology made publishing more attractive to commercial publishers. As a result, "many commercial publishers entered this lucrative market until they surpassed the efforts of scholarly societies and often assumed the publication of these societies' journals."[8] Then, in the 1970s and 1980s, with increased pressure on faculty members to publish, there was yet another upsurge in journal development. Even before that, in the 1960s, Derek de Solla Price observed that:

> The number of journals has behaved just like a
> colony of rabbits breeding among themselves

and reproducing every so often.... Every year about one in twenty, or about 5 percent of the population, had a journal-child ... which must inevitably multiply the population by ten in each succeeding half-century.[9]

The number of scholarly journals currently published is elusive. A 1979 report on scholarly publishing noted that there are no universally applied, unambiguous criteria for distinguishing between scholarly journals on the one hand and trade and professional journals on the other.[10] And the very speed with which new journals are introduced and others cease publication makes it hard to determine the number published at any one moment. In 1988 alone more than 5,000 new journals began publication.[11] *Ulrich's International Periodicals Directory* estimates that in 1989 there were 111,950 periodicals of all kinds in print, almost double the 1978 estimate of 60,000.[12]

Large commercial publishers now dominate the production of scholarly journals: approximately one hundred publishers are now responsible for 70 percent of all journals. The change from the domination of scholarly publishing by universities and professional associations to private publishers may partially account for the increase in the journals published and a rise in journal costs because private firms must show a profit. In just 10 years, from 1977 to 1987, the average cost of a journal increased 110 percent, according to R.T. Lenzini.[13] Rogers and Hurt, looking at an overlapping decade (from 1979 to 1989), reported a higher increase of 160 percent.[14]

Libraries usually pay a higher price for scholarly journals than do individual subscribers, whose membership fee to a professional society often includes the price of a journal sponsored by the society. The higher price charged to libraries is rationalized by publishers because libraries have multiple users and disseminate the information contained in the journals over many years. However, according to Sapp and Watson, the rise in cost of scholarly journals has had adverse effects on all American academic libraries. Orders have been cancelled and new purchases trimmed. The exploding, and apparently unchecked, costs associated with journal acquisition now threaten to outdistance li-

*Robin P. Peek
and Joan N.
Burstyn*

brary budgets.[15]

This increase in journal costs has been particularly burdensome because, in addition to the initial cost of purchasing a journal, an academic library has to spend money on staff time to take each journal subscription through cataloguing, shelving, and storage. The cost in staff time for processing frequently exceeds the initial price of the journal. Beyond the cost of staff time, more money has to be spent for academic journals to be bound into volumes or repurchased in microfilm.

Each journal has to be stored, and space as well as time costs money. An academic library spends a great deal on space that has controlled temperature and humidity for the preservation of paper materials. In 1989 a square foot of library space cost $95.43.[16]

Cost is not the only reason that librarians may hesitate to purchase new journals. Quality is another. In a florid sentence, Lubans questions whether an alternative format, such as electronic journals, will "save us from the heartbreak of scholarly drivel, the embarrassment of book budget bankruptcy, the halitosis of salami publications and the morbid obesity of our collections?"[17]

Not surprisingly, academic libraries are seeking new ways to obtain and store journals. Since libraries have traditionally collected and maintained scholarly information for members of society, any adaptations they choose to make in the selection, format, and storing of journals will significantly impact publishers and scholars.

Alternatives to Traditional Publishing

The search for a more efficient approach to scholarly communication is not exclusive to the information age. Since the 1960s, scholars and librarians have suggested alternatives not only to paper, the medium on which a scholarly article is published, but to the format of the scholarly article itself.

In 1960 a UNESCO Bulletin for Libraries, *Alternatives to the Scientific Periodical*, summarized concerns raised at that time by scholars about the ability of journals and journal-length submissions to meet the information needs of the user:

...the multiplicity of journals results in a scattering of papers which makes it impossible for the scientists to keep informed of new developments, impossible for libraries to cover a field completely, and impossible for abstracting services to include all relevant articles. One writer estimates that a single article in a highly specialized periodical is of interest to only 10 percent of the workers in the subject area covered by the journal, that an article in a general periodical may be of interest to only two percent of its readers, and that an article in a local publication may interest one-quarter of one percent of the scientists in its field. Other writers have said that intense specialization has made it impossible for scientists to read more than a fraction of the articles in journals in their own field... A scientist subscribing to a journal is forced to pay for twenty or thirty papers which do not concern him [sic] in order to get the one paper he wants.[18]

In the years between 1960 and today, specialization has increased, journals have multiplied, and, despite the spread of electronic cataloguing and retrieval services, individual scholars still struggle with the problems identified above.

Micrographics

The first alternative format for scholarly journals resulted from the desire to reduce publishing costs and the need to find a less expensive and more stable storage medium than paper. Some American research libraries began to microfilm valuable collections in the 1930s, and in 1938 University Microfilms International was founded. However, it was not until the late 1950s that micrographics were adopted more widely to preserve deteriorating paper materials and store information at a comparatively low cost with great savings of space.[19] There are two kinds of micrographics: microforms, which include microfilm and microfiche, and the less common microcards.

The first serial research journal exclusively in microform

Robin P. Peek and Joan N. Burstyn

was published in January 1959.[20] The journal, *Wildlife Diseases*, was short-lived; it discontinued publication in the 1970s. The most recent effort occurred in 1980, when the *Bulletin of the Geological Society of America* decided to publish its papers exclusively in microform, only to find its submissions drop precipitately. By 1990, only one journal, the *International Microform Journal of Legal Medicine and Forensic Science*, founded in 1965, was still being published exclusively in microform.[21]

Microforms, primarily microfilm, have, however, evolved as secondary publishing media for many journals originally published in paper. Secondary services, such as University Microforms International, a journal and magazine clearinghouse, will republish annual collections of journals for academic libraries on microforms. They have the advantage of reduced size for storage, a more stable medium, and elimination of the need to bind journals in their original paper format.

Despite the advantages of microforms for librarians, scholars find problems using them. They have to be read with a microform reader. Unlike books, their content cannot easily be photocopied and annotated. While moderately priced portable microform readers are available, few scholars buy one for personal use. There are rarely sufficient journals and documents on microform available for individual subscription in any field to warrant such an expenditure. If a scholar purchases a microform reader, he or she still needs to print copies of documents in order to annotate them, and that has to be done where a microform printer is available. Frequently the cost of microform copies exceeds that of photocopies of paper journals even though the copies may be of poorer quality.

Separates (Selective Dissemination of Information)

The production of separates (or SDIs in micrographics) addresses two complaints frequently lodged against traditional journals: that they take too long to make material available, and that only one or two articles in a particular issue of a journal may interest each reader. Separates may be viewed as "tailor made" journals. The Society of Automotive Engineers, which began to publish separates in 1965, is one of the few organizations still continuing the practice today. The society stocks separate papers for three years. They may be ordered individually or in microfiche sets. The society has ceased publishing a conventional journal.

SDI services were also attempted by the American Mathematical Society, the Institute of Electrical and Electronic Engineers, the American Institute of Aeronautics and Astronautics, and the American Chemical Society. All were unsuccessful. According to the Report of the National Enquiry on Scholarly Communication, the IEEE experiment failed because engineers were unwilling to purchase individual articles on a regular basis.[22] The report also suggests that the "single journal article may be too small a unit to be sold economically because of the large transaction costs involved."[23]

Synopsis Journals

A synopsis journal is a hybrid of the traditional journal and an SDI. Synopsis journals were introduced primarily to cope with an oversupply of manuscripts.[24] Articles in synopsis journals are refereed, but the journals restrict print publication to a synopsis (or long summary) of the original manuscript. Complete manuscripts are provided on request as an additional service.[25]

Beginning in the late 1960s, the Institution of Mechanical Engineers, the Geological Society of America, the Royal Society of Chemistry, and the American Institute of Aeronautics and Astronautics all experimented with synopsis journals. A variation of the synopsis journal was begun by the *Journal of Modern History*, which from 1975 to 1981 published in microfiche some extra-long articles that otherwise would have been excluded from the journal in its paper format. Most synopsis journals, however, met with limited success; they either ceased publication or continued in limited form. Scholars expressed concern over uncertain refereeing standards and, as a result, research in synopsis journals was branded second-rate.

*Robin P. Peek
and Joan N.
Burstyn*

The Move Toward Electronic Publishing

The first experiments in publishing electronically information that traditionally was printed occurred in the late 1960s, when bibliographic information services (secondary publishers) began publishing electronic versions of print indexes. Indexes are particularly attractive in an electronic format because they lend themselves to the search capabilities of the computer and their value is enhanced by the speed with which they are made available.

In its early years, electronic publishing depended on the formation of databases accessed through mainframe computers, and readers were limited to those scholars with access to mainframes. The data bases accessed through mainframe computers were said to be on-line. Although the readership was small at first, these experiments demonstrated that computers could be an excellent vehicle for delivering information.

In the late 1970s vendors began to combine bibliographic files with abstracts. In an offhand way, this created a type of electronic synopsis journal. The move blurred the distinction between primary and secondary publishers and created new concerns, such as who owns the abstracts of texts.

There are now three main vendors to academic institutions of on-line information: Dialog, BRS, and Wilson Publishing. These private firms provide the bulk of the commercial on-line services. Their files now range in the thousands, with hundreds being added each year. They have recently expanded their services to include not only bibliographic information, but numeric and full-text retrieval. In growing numbers, newspapers and magazines are simultaneously offering on-line the text from their print publishing. Wang refers to the joint publication of journals in both print and electronic format as parallel publishing. He distinguishes parallel publishing from publication only in electronic form, for which he reserves the term electronic publishing. [26]

In parallel publishing, instead of purchasing a print copy a user or library may pay a fee to the vendor of the on-line service for each article viewed or printed. However, at the moment the fee frequently exceeds the cost of purchasing the entire printed publication containing the article. Today, the same versions of many scientific and technical journals are available both on-line and in print.

Experiments in the Exclusively Electronic Journal

A scholarly journal published electronically has the potential to overcome many problems associated with paper publication. By eliminating printing and distribution time, papers can be published faster. Since printing and mailing costs are eliminated, restrictions on the size of journals can be lifted. In theory, at least, the costs of publishing should decrease and so should the cost of journal subscriptions.

There are, of course, problems to be considered. Indexing services still form the backbone of scholarly dissemination. However, indexing has traditionally been a selective process. An index is not required, or expected, to include every work that is published. As a result, scholars frequently complain about the incompleteness of indexing services.

Another problem, arising from both the ability to provide full-text retrieval and a forum for papers longer than those printed, is that instead of reading the abstract of a paper, or the whole of a short one, a scholar may be forced to sift through ones that are hundreds of pages long. This is not only time consuming but could be very costly if charges were assigned by the page. Another concern with a wealth of material is that the role of scholars as editors, reviewers, and managers of journals will become much more onerous.

The first application of electronic technology to scholarly journals was proposed in the 1970s as part of larger experiments in electronic communication.[27] These were undertaken in the United States with the Electronic Information Exchange System (EIES), in the United Kingdom with the Birmingham and Loughborough Electronic Network Development (BLEND), and in Canada with COMTEX. None of these experiments was entirely successful, most did not last long, and only part of the original EIES still continues. According to Piternick, only two issues of the electronic journal sponsored by BLEND, and one is-

*Robin P. Peek
and Joan N.
Burstyn*

sue of the journal sponsored by COMTEX were published. Those running the journals reported, however, that their experience of collaborating with others on the project was important to them.[28] (Since such collaboration will increase as electronic communication becomes more common, its impact on those involved is a fertile topic for further study.[29]) In all three experiments, researchers encountered resistance to electronic journals from the scientific community. Some objected to the format; some expressed concern that the quality control and the review process were inadequate. In addition, the experiments were constrained by the limitations of computer technology and scholars' computer literacy at the time.

In 1984, Learned Information Ltd. introduced *The Electronic Magazine*, composed of previously unpublished works in electronic format. The following year, Information Access Companies mounted an experiment called *Information Publishing: An Electronic Journal*, which became a model for later electronic journals. These two appealed to a general not a scholarly audience and one predisposed to electronic publishing.

Two scenarios for the future of electronic journals have been suggested. In the first, the public becomes so accustomed to on-line journals that publishers abandon paper versions altogether. There is some debate whether distribution would remain on-line exclusively or if supplementary forms of distribution, such as providing disks or alternative hard copy print-outs, would be needed.

In the second scenario, individual subscriptions to journals come to an end. Individual papers are held in a massive centralized data base that the user accesses via telecommunications. The user is charged a fee for use of individual papers or records. Rogers and Hurt describe such a system, the Scholarly Communication System, an electronic network on which scholars in all disciplines could publish as well as read other publications. They describe the publication process as follows:

As a scholar completed an article or paper, it would be sent electronically to the system, where it would be assigned a category and cross-referenced to other relevant categories.... The system could provide three new capabilities: a "notes and comments" section, citation tracking, and a usage log. Scholars with valid passwords, obtained by paying a modest annual fee, could leave signed statements related to the article's content. The system would be available 22 hours a day to anyone paying the hourly usage and printing charges.[30]

An article would be reviewed only after it had been in the system for six months and had been subjected to comments made electronically by scholars in the field. The author would then be notified that she or he had ten working days to prepare a final version. If the author failed to do so, the article would be removed from the system.

Under this plan, each discipline (or interdisciplinary) group would have its own review board and management whose members would be nominated and elected by participating institutions. The review boards would perform the same tasks as editors of current scholarly journals.

In 1990, the PSYCOLOQUY discussion group, an electronic network of psychologists, examined a plan similar to that put forward by Rogers and Hurt, from William P. Gardner.[31] In a paper from *Psychological Science*, the abstract of which he posted on the network, Gardner suggested "the primary advantage of electronic publishing is not the inexpensive delivery of text, but the use of a centralized archive to concentrate resources for discovering and utilizing information" and outlined ways such an archive might function.[32] In the discussion that followed, Mani Ganesh, of the University of Wisconsin, suggested each field have a MEGAJOURNAL for communicating and archiving research, with a pyramid of refereed outlets. The MEGAJOURNAL could serve as a clearinghouse both for articles and for conference and workshop papers. According to Ganesh, "the centralized storage of information will be something of a dream come true for researchers trying to find technical, up-to-date, detailed in-

*Robin P. Peek
and Joan N.
Burstyn*

formation about a particular project." As Francis C. Dane of Mercer University pointed out later in the discussion, print journals proliferated because each one had a limit on its space. An electronic journal has no such limitation; it can publish *all* the research in a given field.

David S. Stodolsky, whose response to Gardner was also printed in *Psychological Science*, was alarmed at the prospect of centralization. He argued, first, that electronic publishing will lead to "qualitative changes in scientific communication," and, second, that the intellectual goals of individual users will be served best by a decentralized system of publishing and archiving. Citing F.C. Michel, Stodolsky claimed that only the logic of a scientific argument should determine its influence and that the "power relations inherent in the operation of a preview journal contradict this ideal."[33] Stodolsky believes that a new medium, a mix of electronic mail and electronic publishing, could evolve if scientific societies accepted their responsibility to shape it. J.A. Pickering of the University of Warwick responded with the argument that rapid editorial and peer response "may in turn permit the contents of electronic journals to be more like the record of a dialogue in progress rather that the interchange of [re]latively finalized positions."

Stodolsky also called for scientists to look critically at existing norms within their disciplines whereby "stars" who become famous "can then be 'bought' by publishers who [put] their names on the mastheads of journals." Stodolsky feels that both scientists and the general public will suffer if the social organization of science does not change in response to the new media.

The scenarios identified above suggest an abrupt departure from traditional scholarly communication. Both raise the specter of new problems for scholars or the exacerbation of ones already encountered with the forms of communication described earlier in this chapter.

One problem is how scholars will deal with an increase in the amount of reading they have to do. Because it is cheaper to produce and distribute than a paper version, the electronic journal could empower scholars to write more and longer research articles. As we mentioned with regard to separates and SDIs, another problem likely to emerge is quality control. Not only must scholars be concerned about the quality of papers from the perspective of consumers; they must also consider their roles as peer reviewers and editors. How will they deal with pressure to review more articles? Will the role of editor become more or less arduous? How will it change? If restrictions to publication based on cost are lifted, what will stop the publication of second- and third-rate work? Will the very notion of a journal, in which several papers are collected and published together, be abandoned?

If all publication on paper is eliminated, scholars' relationship to research libraries will change dramatically. Scholars will have individual access through their computers to catalogs and indexes; they will no longer have to rely on those developed by librarians for print media. On the other hand, they will still need assistance in identifying and selecting source materials. Who will conduct the new types of cataloguing, classifying, and indexing—librarians, electronic publishers, or secondary publishers? Who will assist scholars to identify and select source material—resource people from libraries, from academic computing services, or from on-line service vendors? And will scholars still expect libraries to generate and store paper or microform copies of electronic materials? As Eldred Smith has pointed out recently, computer technology has made it possible, for the first time, to preserve the whole scholarly record.[34] Yet this same technology also makes possible the informal distribution of new publications whose identification, collection, and preservation have become more difficult.

Electronic Journals and the Scholarly Community

Electronic publishing has problems similar to those posed by microforms: the use of a monitor for reading is less desirable than the use of a book. As the Report of the National Enquiry on Scholarly Communication stated: "User resistance to the substitution of micofilm or microfiche for books remains strong."[35] Similarly, Wang has reported with regard to reading from a computer screen:

> Physically, it is uncomfortable to read long texts on a screen. It is also inconvenient to read elec-

*Robin P. Peek
and Joan N.
Burstyn*

tronic publications because of the need of equipment for reading and because of the rather large size of the equipment. In respect of the ability of display on a screen, it is still limited in presenting graphics, color, special letters, signs and symbols. It is especially inconvenient to lay out on a screen several pages at the same time for the purpose of comparison.[36]

Users are also concerned for the stability and ease of use of electronic media. Unlike microforms, the standard size and format for electronic media have yet to be established. For libraries this is a serious issue because long-term storage is a key consideration. Obviously a medium that can be accessed only by a particular type of obsolete equipment can cripple the holdings of a library. Just as the 5 1/4 inch computer disk is being replaced by the 3 1/2 inch disk, the size of CD-ROMs may change, and no one can predict when a standard will be arrived at.

Microform technology is comparatively straightforward compared to computing. Microform readers are not subject to going "down" for hours or days at a time, as sometimes occurs with libraries' CD-ROM and computer equipment. Though academic libraries have multiple microform readers, they are unlikely to have spare CD-ROM readers.

Another concern with electronic publishing is cost. In spite of current subsidies from academic libraries, on-line services are frequently provided for a fee that is charged the individual or the department. The scholarly community blanches at the notion of user fees, and with good reason. The most intense use of scholarly journals is by graduate students and untenured faculty members, those in the poorest position to pay fees. While no study has shown how scholars use the information they obtain on-line, their concern over the accuracy of citations suggests that they would need to have copies of the works and would thus resist having to work from a purely electronic format. This, in turn, means that libraries or academic departments become mini-publishers generating specific "separates" for their users.

Despite the apparent ease and efficiency of electronic

information transfer, faculty access to individual workstations is not widespread. Adjunct faculty in particular are rarely given such access. Yet, for electronic publishing to be effective, most if not all scholars and teachers would need access, not only to a computer, but to a telecommunications system that would interact with the host information sources.

A related problem is that monitors of a size and resolution for effective viewing are typically not available to most faculty members. In part this is due to the age of the equipment many faculty members are using. Even fewer have access to color monitors. And, as mentioned above, one of the critical problems is that scholars find it uncomfortable to read text on computer screens for extended periods. Consequently there will probably be a continuing desire among scholars to print out papers for both ease of reading and for annotation. This threatens to be a tremendous financial burden for the university or for individual scholars.

Though we may be in the computer age, computer use among faculty members is not universal. Some observers speculate that most faculty members are only marginally literate in computer use and limit themselves to word processing. To educate them further about the potential of computers for teaching and research would mean an expensive educational process.

Until everyone in the academic community embraces computing, many editors will remain uncomfortable with publishing scholarly work electronically, as will scholars be reluctant to publish through it. This reaction parallels that made to earlier attempts to deviate from traditional forms of publishing. Thus, the tendency will be for scholars to publish through traditional channels first, because the status of traditional journals is understood by those responsible for promotion and tenure decisions. Electronic journals, unless add-ons to print, will most likely be considered only by those established scholars who wish to experiment or by those who are unsuccessful in publishing their work elsewhere. Exceptions to this are scholars engaged in artificial intelligence and cognitive psychology, both burgeoning fields, who have chosen to publish their work

In Pursuit of
Improved
Scholarly
Communications

*Robin P. Peek
and Joan N.
Burstyn*

electronically via personal computers.[37] It is questionable whether these scholars could lead the rest of the academic community into electronic publishing, however. They may, like those in computer science itself, be considered anomalies because of their strong connection with computers and their lack of a tradition of paper publications.

A strong argument for electronic publishing is that it could reduce costs of production. A unique incentive for the primary publisher today is that the majority of all text submitted to scholarly journals is created on a word processor and submitted on disk with instructions for printing already keyed into it. Small publishers particularly have come to rely on this as a way to save money on typesetting manuscripts. Kennedy suggests that this change in the way manuscripts are submitted is due both to economics and to the more significant use of computers for composition and editing. However, there is a difference between preparing manuscripts electronically for publication in print and distributing them electronically. Some authors claim that the cost of computer inputting and distribution will remain too high to make electronic publishing feasible on a large scale.[38] Astle contends that:

> Electronic journals, especially if produced as refereed titles by commercial publishers, would not be less expensive than the printed versions, as the costs for peer review, article compositions, editorial work, etc. would be similar. Only the costs for the actual printing could be eliminated. Publishers would still require a profit, though they may earn it on a per-article basis rather than through subscriptions, or they may set a combination price with an access fee to provide a steady income and a separate charge for each article used.[39]

Other authors have suggested establishing a corporation to meet the bulk of the costs. For example, Rogers and Hurt foresee that the $500 million spent annually on journal subscriptions could finance their suggested Scholarly Communication System.[40] The capital for the organization would be provided by grants and fees from universities, foundations, and government agencies. Annual subscription fees would pay for administrative costs, honoraria, and expenses. Annual fees would be assessed on a sliding scale, based on the programs offered at a particular college or university. The authors estimate that universities would spend substantially less through this system than they currently spend on subscriptions, although they make no statements regarding the project's annual costs.

Whatever the wishes of scholars or research libraries, Simpson foresees that they will have little choice in how the publishing industry chooses to package and price its wares. He predicts that three tiers of information will evolve: information with commercial value to business, industry, science, and technology, which will be converted to and stored in digitized form; useful facts and popular entertainment, which will be available on videodisks or in so-called electronic books; and information in print format which will be considered less interesting and useful, and will be in low demand.[41]

Conclusion

Despite efforts over the past 30 years to change the process of scholarly communication, the tradition of print-on-paper publication in refereed journals is still entrenched in the scholarly community. Few past experiments to reduce production costs and improve communications have resulted in lasting changes.

Libraries, not individuals, are the main purchasers of scholarly works. This is because the task of preserving scholarship and making it available to scholars has belonged to the academic library. Therefore, unless new means are found to preserve the scholarly record and make it available to all, the provision of ways to view and store electronic publishing will become the responsibility of the library and not the individual scholar.[42]

Paper publishing is both profitable and a format that scholars and libraries still prefer. The integration of electronic publishing into scholarly communication could, therefore, be gradual and not revolutionary as is so often threatened.

Historically, the academic community has been conser-

*Robin P. Peek
and Joan N.
Burstyn*

vative. Scholarly traditions, passed down to new scholars for generations, are slow to change. And so, despite the complaints, the current system of scholarly publishing may remain the one that works best for scholars. The solution to the complaints of scholars may lie in changing the reward structure for academics not in changing the system of scholarly publishing. If the requirement for university scholars to publish or perish is producing unacceptable research, it may be time to change the requirement. With its ability for whole text storage and retrieval, the new communications technology has already highlighted shortcomings in the academic reward structure.

As publishing moves into an electronic format, caution needs to be exercised lest the quality control mechanisms of scholarly communication be destroyed entirely. As John Ziman has commented, the role of referees in scholarly publishing is a source of contention,

> yet we cannot dispense with some such system, for it is essential that the material to be found in the "archival literature" of science should at least seem honest and plausible to those capable of assessing it at the time. The mere fact that an author has a Ph.D.—or is even a distinguished professor—does not ensure that he [sic] is free from bias, folly, error, or even mild insanity.[43]

Ziman's comment applies to all fields of scholarship, not merely science. If existing quality control mechanisms are destroyed and not replaced by similar ones, electronic data bases may become scholarly flea markets.

Dramatic change is in the wind, however. There are many players involved with the new technology and profits to be made from its expansion. Reluctant though scholars may be, change may be forced upon them by the publishing and computer industries.

The cost of changing to an electronic environment will be high. All parties affected by the changing technology will have to share in bearing that cost. As there is a fair-use provision in the copyright law, perhaps a similar system for the use of on-line services could be devised to allow colleges and universities to adapt efficiently. No one will benefit if academia is forced to starve for information. In the past, publishers adapted their price structures to the realities of having most scholarly books and journals purchased by libraries; in the future, they will have to provide information electronically at an affordable price, even if that means finding new ways to package information for scholars in higher education.

In Pursuit of Improved Scholarly Communications

NOTES

1. John Lubans, Jr., "Scholars and Serials," *American Libraries* 18, no. 3 (March 1987): 180.

2. Anne B. Piternick, "Attempts to Find Alternatives to the Scientific Journal: A Brief Review," *Journal of Academic Librarianship* 15, no 5, (1989): 263.

3. David C. Taylor, *Managing The Serials Explosion* (New York: Knowledge Industry Publications, 1982), p. 10.

4. *Ibid.*

5. Derek J. de Solla Price, *Little Science, Big Science* (New York: Columbia University Press, 1963), p.63.

6. Donald Case, "The Personal Computer: Missing Link to the Electronic Journal," *Journal of the American Society for Information Science* 36, no. 5 (198): 309-313.

7. John Ziman, "Information, Communication, Knowledge," *Nature* 224 (October 25, 1969): 318.

8. Deana L. Astle, "The Scholarly Journal: Whence or Wither," *Journal of Academic Librarianship* 15, no. 3 (1989): 152.

9. Derek de Solla Price, *Science Since Babylon* (New Haven: Yale University Press, 1975. Original copyright, 1961.), p. 170.

10. See National Enquiry into Scholarly Communication, *Scholarly Communication: The Report of the National Enquiry* (Baltimore, MD: Johns Hopkins University Press, 1979), p. 39.

11. See Sharon J. Rogers and Charlene S. Hurt, "How Scholarly Communication Should work in the 21st Century," *Chronicle of Higher Education* 36, no. 7 (1989), A56.

*Robin P. Peek
and Joan N.
Burstyn*

12. See *Ulrich's International Periodical Directory* 1988-1989 (New York: Bowker, 1989), p. vii.

13. See Rebecca T. Lenzini, "Periodical Prices: 1985-87 Update," *Serials Librarian* 13 (September, 1987): 49-57.

14. See Rogers and Hurt, "How Scholarly Communication Should Work,": A56.

15. See Gregg Sapp and Peter G. Watson, "Library Relations During a Period of Journal Cancellations," *Journal of Academic Librarianship* 15, no. 5 (November 1989): 285-289.

16. See Rogers and Hurt, "How Scholarly Communication Should Work,": A56.

17. Lubans, "Scholars and Serials,": 180.

18. Ralph H. Phelps and John P. Herlin, *Alternatives to the Scientific Periodical: A Report and Bibliography*, UNESCO Bulletin for Libraries 14 (March-April 1960), p. 62, as quoted in Astle, "The Scholarly Journal," p. 151-52. (Eight citations originally in this quotation are omitted by Astle. They are identified briefly in Phelps and Herlin, p.62 and in more detail, pp. 71-75.)

19. See Richard M. Dougherty, "Year's Work in Acquisitions," *Library Resources and Technical Service* 9, no. 2 (Spring, 1965): 149-156; and Ralph J. Folcarelli, Arthur C. Tannenbaum, and Ralph C. Ferragamo, *The Microform Connection: A Basic Guide For Libraries* (New York: R. R. Bowker Company, 1982)pp. 5-7.

20. See H.E. Kennedy, "Information Delivery Options Over Three Decades," *Information Services and Use* 6, no. 4 (1986): 135-51.

21. See Phelps and Herlin, *Alternatives to the Scientific Periodical*, p. 62; and Piternick, "Attempts to Find Alternatives,": 263.

22. See *Scholarly Communication*, p. 75.

23. *Ibid.*

24. *Ibid.*

25. See Piternick, "Attempts to Find Alternatives,": 262.

26. See Chih Wang, "Electronic Publishing and Its Impact," *Electronic Publishing Review* 6, no.1 (1986): 43-55.

27. See Alan Singleton, "The Electronic Journal and Its Relatives," *Scholarly Publishing* 13, no.3 (October 1981): 3-18.

28. See Piternick, "Attempts to Find Alternatives,": 263-64.

29. A suggestion on how to measure adult learning during collaborative work (although in a different setting) may be found in an unpublished paper by Rae W. Rohfeld and Joan N. Burstyn of Syracuse University, "New Perspectives on Community and Self: Implications of Constructing History—A Case Study," (1990).

30. See Rogers and Hurt, "How Scholarly Communication Should Work,": A56.

31. PSYCOLOQUY (psych@tcsvm), an electronic discussion group sponsored by the Science Directorate of the American Psychological Association, has an elaborate hierarchy moderating its discussions: two coeditors, Stevan Harnad, Princeton University, and Perry London, Rutgers, the State University of New Jersey; an associate editor, Cary Cherniss, Rutgers; and two assistant editors, Malcolm Baur, Princeton, and John Pizutelli, Rutgers. Although the group's discussion takes the form of E-mail messages, these are posted in groups and titled by volume and issue as is typical for a journal. The format for discussion and for referring to previous comments is evolving and has become more formalized each month.

The material cited in the chapter was obtained October 16, 1990, and refers to William P. Gardner's comments in volume 1, Issue 8 (May 25, 1990). A later presentation, in the traditional format of a paper, by David S. Stodolsky on "Consensus Journals: Invitational Journals Based Upon Peer Consensus," may be found in Volume VI, #15 (Discussion of E-Journals), November 19, 1990.

In this chapter, names of the discussion participants have been inserted as appropriate into the text.

32. See William P. Gardner, "Scientific Publishing for the 90's," and an invited comment on the paper by D. Stodolsky, *Psychological Science* (1990): in press. The abstract and discussion were posted in PSYCOLOQUY vol. 1: Issue 8.

33. Stodolsky cites F.C. Michel, "Solving the Problem of Refereeing," *Physics Today* 9, (1982): 82.

34. See Eldred Smith, *The Librarian, the Scholar, and the Future of the Research Library* (New York: Greenwood Press, 1990), pp. 29-40.

*Robin P. Peek
and Joan N.
Burstyn*

35. *Scholarly Communication*, p.4.

36. Wang, "Electronic Publishing and Its Impact,": 47.

37. See Thomas W. Shaughnessy, "Scholarly Communication: The Need for an Agenda for Action," *Journal of Academic Librarianship* 15, no.2 (May 1989): 68-71.

38. See Lubans, "Scholars and Serials,": 180.

39. Astle, "The Scholarly Journal,": 153-54.

40. See Rogers and Hurt, "How Scholarly Communication Should Work,": A56.

41. Jack Simpson as quoted in "Simpson Sees Emergence of Worldwide Electronic Megalibrary," *Advanced Technology Libraries* 14, no. 9, (June 1985): 4.

42. See Smith, *The Librarian, the Scholar, and the Future of the Research Library*, chapter 5.

43. John M. Ziman, *The Force of Knowledge: The Scientific Dimension of Society* (Cambridge: Cambridge University Press, 1976), p.104.

NOTE ON THE AUTHORS

Joan N. Burstyn is Professor of Cultural Foundations of Education, and of History, Syracuse University

Charles L. Creesy is Computer Administrator, Princeton University Press

Czeslaw Jan Grycz is Chairman, Scholarship and Technology Project, University of California

Robert M. Hayes is Professor of Library and Information Science, University of California, Los Angeles

Deborah G. Johnson is Professor of Philosophy, Department of Science and Technical Studies, Rensselaer Polytechnic Institute

David May is Executive Director, Publications, Printing, and Graphic Services, Syracuse University

Robert L. Oakman is Professor of Computer Science, University of South Carolina

Robin P. Peek is End-User Consultant, Academic Computing Services, and a Doctoral Student in Higher Education, Syracuse University

Robert J. Silverman is Professor of Education, Ohio State University, and Editor of the *Journal of Higher Education*

INDEX

PSYCOLOQUY, 109-10
PSYCOLOQUY
(psch@tcsvm), 119n31
Publication process, 48-49
    for conference proceedings,
    25-26
Publish!, 10, 91
Publishers
    authors' responsibilities
    to, 86
    role of, 27-29, 38
    views on, 85-86
Publishing
    def. of, 47-48
    in the Middle Ages, 51
    parallel, 106-7
    process of, 80-82
    changes in, 11
    technology's role, 80
    traditional, 115
    alternatives to, 102-3
Publishing business, 4-5
    changes in, 71-72
    compared to scholarly
    publishing, 79-82
    concentration in, 100-1
Purpose (of text), 3, 11

Q

Quality, 57-58. *see also* Control;
    Issues; Standards
    of electronic review, 58
    function of review, 70-71
    of scholarly journals, 102
    threats to, 79
Quality control, 50-51, 116. *see*
    also Control; Peer review;
    Standards in book
    publication, 37
    expert systems for, 42-43
    issues, 18
    publisher role in, 28
    threats to, 40
Questionnaire, electronic,
    15-16

R

"... rabbits breeding," 100-1
Readability, 81, 112. *see also*
    Formatting and layout;
    Legibility screen, 15
Reader/author
    communication, 57
Reading repertoires, 59
Realities/possibilities, created
    by computers, 65-69
Refereeing. *see also* Peer review
    of desktop publications, 29
Referees' role, in electronic
    discourse, 57-58
*Report of the National Enquiry
on Scholarly Communication*
    (1979), 111
    on IEEE experiment, 105
Report publication, 31-32
Reports, joint, 29-30
Research. *see also* Scholarly
    communication
    evaluation of, 30-31
    reporting standards for, 58
    screening of, 43-44
    in synopsis journals, 105
    vs. teaching, 11-12, 21n11
Research library. *see* Libraries
Resistance to change, 69
Responsibilities. *see also* Roles
    of authors, 79
    to publishers, 86
    of the library, 31-33
    of publisher, 28
Revenue gain, 93
Reviewer reaction, 63n18
Revision "following
    publication," 58
Revolutionary. *see also* Change
    aspects, 19
    def. of, 66
    potential of technology, 69

Reward structure. *see*
Promotion and tenure

Rigor and integrity, 58

Rogers, Sharon J., 108-9,
114-15

Roles
computer center vs. library,
82
of discourse communities,
58
of editors, 81
of journals, 99
of librarians, 82
of library, 82
of marketing staff, 81
of middle-man/woman,
84-85
peer group, 29-30
at Princeton University
Press, 95-97
publisher, 27-29
of referees, 57-59, 116
of technology, 80

Royal Society of Chemistry,
105

S

Scholarly communication. *see
also* Discourse communities;
Peer review;
Research; Scholarly journal
control of, 43-44
dangers to, 30-31
and electronic review,
63n18
evolution of, 80
history of, 99-102
problems in, 99
publisher role in, 27-29
and referee process, 116
system view of, 80-82
traditional vs. new, 8-9

Scholarly Communication,
Report on (1979), 101,
105, 111

Scholarly Communication
System, 108-9, 114

Scholarly community
conservatism of, 115-16
and electronic journals,
111-15

Scholarly journal. *see also*
Electronic journal;
Scholarly communication
alternatives to, 103-5
average cost of, 101
count of, 101
def. of, 99-101
inadequacy of, 102-3
micrographic, 103-4
proliferation of, 100-1
role of, 99
specialization of, 103

Scholarly process. *see*
Scholarly communication

Scholars, community of, 56

Scholarship, quality of, 18

*Science and Technology
Studies*, 57-58

Science in Action, 58-59

Screen readability, 15, 112

Screening of scholarly
research, 43-44

SDIs in micrographics,
104-5, 111

Secondary publishers, 106

Selection and acquisition, of
desktop publications, 32

Selective Dissemination of
Information. *see* Separates
(Selective Dissemination of
Information)

Separates (Selective
Dissemination of
Information), 104-5, 110

Serials problem, 99. *see also*
Costs;
Proliferation of journals

SGML (Structured
Generalized Markup
Language), 87

Silverman, Robert J., 14